Finally Laid to Rest

The work of a real UK

'Cold Case' Review Team

by

Ray Newman

ISBN-13: 978-1523857135

ISBN-10: 1523857137

DEDICATION

This book is dedicated
to the victims of the crimes, etc., detailed within it
and to their families and friends.

ACKNOWLEDGMENTS

I WOULD LIKE TO ACKNOWLEDGE
ALL THE HARD WORK CARRIED OUT BY
POLICE OFFICERS AND POLICE SUPPORT STAFF,
FORENSIC SCIENTISTS,
CROWN PROSECUTORS AND COUNSEL.

THIS HAS ENABLED SOME OF THOSE
WHO COMMITTED THE MOST SERIOUS CRIMES
TO BE BROUGHT TO JUSTICE
DESPITE THE PASSAGE OF TIME.

MORE CONVICTIONS WILL UNDOUBTEDLY FOLLOW!

CONTENTS

CHAPTER 1
INTRODUCTION

I am a retired Detective Chief Inspector, later to become a founding member of the Essex Police Major Crime Review Team. This book provides an insight into just some of our work.

When sixty three year-old Rochford shopkeeper Norah Trott stepped through her front door and out into the street on that dark, dank, November evening in 1978, she had no reason to fear for her safety. Norah's route would take her up Old Ship Lane, illuminated by street lamps and the light exuding from two public houses on either side of the lane. There was also the occasional firework, for it was the evening following Guy Fawkes Night.

Norah had no way of knowing that she was about to be savagely beaten and brutally raped by a complete stranger; nor, as she lay dying, that it would take 'Cold Case' officers more than twenty five years to catch her killer.

Similarly, a sudden, violent death was the last thing eighteen year-old student Dinah McNicol could have expected as she hitch-hiked home along the busy A3 trunk road in Surrey.

Dinah lived with her family in Tillingham, a village not far from Chelmsford, Essex. On the 5th August 1991, having spent the weekend at a music festival in Liphook, Hampshire, Dinah began her journey home. She was hitch-hiking with a young man she had only met that weekend and both were travelling in the same direction to their respective homes; at least for part of their journeys. They gladly accepted a lift from a middle aged man, who later dropped Dinah's travelling companion at Junction 8 of the M25 Motorway in Surrey. Dinah was only an hour or two from home and would surely have arrived safely, had they not accepted a lift from serial killer Peter Tobin.

Dinah failed to arrive home, but her disappearance was not immediately realised. But once it was, police launched a missing person's investigation. After examining bank records they discovered that all Dinah's savings, which in theory only she could access, had already been withdrawn from various automatic cash machines along the south coast of England.

Had Dinah decided to start a new life elsewhere?

Sadly, it would take well over a decade to recover Dinah's body from a makeshift grave in the back garden of a Margate house; a garden that had also become the resting place of missing Scottish schoolgirl, Vicky Hamilton.

All three killings were committed by complete strangers. But one of the sad facts about murder generally is that many victims are killed by people quite close to them; often people who love or at least, once loved them. Was the murder of Jean Dicker such a case?

On the 29th January 2003, this fifty eight year-old widow and retired traffic warden was beaten to death in the Clacton bungalow she shared with her son, Steven. That evening Steven had gone out to visit a friend, but on returning home he found his mother lying on the hallway floor. She had been savagely beaten to death.

There was no sign of a forced entry to the bungalow, so had Jean been killed by someone she knew, a relative, a friend; or perhaps someone else invited into her home?

But Jean's handbag and mobile telephone were then found to be missing, so was this actually a burglary that had gone horribly wrong?

It took over a year for investigators to find out what had really happened that evening; and to bring Jean's killer to justice.

Similarly, Violet Dunderdale's killer was possibly no stranger to her. Violet was an independent, seventy seven year-old widow who lived alone in a house on the outskirts of Chelmsford. Violet was close to her son Peter, his wife Patricia (known as Pat) and their son Edward (known as Eddie), who unfortunately suffered from Schizophrenia.

Peter's family lived just around the corner from Violet and they would often all go out together for a drink at the local social club. The evening of Sunday 26th July 1999, was no different, except that Peter was in Canada visiting his other two sons.

After their evening out, Pat walked Violet to her home before returning to her own house.

Early the following morning, Eddie woke his mother up telling her that he had just found his grandmother's house insecure. He said he had gone into the house and found his grandmother dead in bed. She had been savagely beaten around the head.

Police were called and shortly after their arrival Eddie was arrested on suspicion of murder. He was taken to Chelmsford Police Station, but soon after his arrival he allegedly began to hear voices, so medical advice was sought. He was sectioned under the Mental Health Act and then admitted to a secure mental hospital. A file of evidence was later considered by the Crown Prosecution Service (CPS) who concluded that there was insufficient evidence to charge Eddie with any offences.

For several years Eddie remained a compulsory in-patient. However, his condition allegedly improved and in 2005, he was released into the care of the community mental health team. But police began to receive reports about his allegedly strange behavior in public. If Eddie really was Violet's killer, he may now pose a very real threat to others. An urgent 'Cold Case' review of Violet's murder was ordered and this finally led to Violet's killer being identified and convicted.

It may seem a strange thing to say, but the families of Dinah McNicol and Vicky Hamilton were fortunate in that at least their bodies were eventually found and returned to them. But, unfortunately, every year thousands of people go missing in the United Kingdom and many are never found. Most families and friends of missing persons are comforted by the fact that the missing person (or as they are known by the police, the MISPER) is normally capable of looking after themselves.

Those relatives and friends may not always know or understand why the MISPER suddenly disappeared. But they have a reasonable expectation that their loved one will soon be found by the police, or will be seen by someone who knows them, or that they will eventually return home of their own accord. But some families seem to know, almost from the outset, that something terrible has happened to their loved ones; and that they are probably already dead.

Relatives' fears may be due to the unusual circumstances of the disappearance. It may have been totally unexpected, out of character, involve the apparent abandonment of young children, dependants, work or other responsibilities. Believing that a missing loved one is dead is bad enough; but never being able to find them or to finally lay them to rest prolongs the agony for a lifetime. Occasionally, police will share a family's concerns to the extent that the MISPER investigation soon becomes a 'No Body' murder investigation.

Over the years there have been a number of such cases in Essex; like that of twenty nine year-old mother of two and bride-to-be Nicola Ray. She vanished from her Pitsea home after a 'girl's night out' one Bank Holiday Monday in 2000. According to her fiancée Tim, Nicola was asleep when he went off to work the following morning; but she was not home when he returned.

The next day Tim went to work as usual, but on returning home he found that Nicola was still absent. Also, that some of her personal possessions were now missing. Had Nicola returned home to collect her things while her fiancée was at work; and was she now living a new life, perhaps hundreds of miles away?

Detectives were soon leading the investigation into Nicola's disappearance, but despite nationwide appeals and extensive enquiries, they could find no trace of her.

Sometimes, formal reviews of historic MISPER investigations finally resolve them (as happened in the case of Dinah McNicol). Consequently, it was felt that even though there was no fresh information about Nicola's disappearance, a 'Cold Case' review might possibly move the investigation forward. It was 2009, and the tenth anniversary of Nicola's disappearance was fast approaching. It was time to look at the case once again. We did; and some progress was indeed made.

Although reviews of unsolved murders take priority, Essex Police, in common with most police forces around the United Kingdom, also reviews other unsolved serious crimes, such as 'Stranger Rapes'.

As the name implies, 'Stranger Rapes' are committed by offenders who are invariably complete strangers to their victims, albeit that their paths may have previously, albeit briefly, crossed. A number of such cases are recounted in this book, including those resulting in the rapists being imprisoned many years after they had committed their crimes. They include the 1993 rape of a Colchester woman walking home alone after a night out; and the 1997 rape of a fifteen year-old Harlow girl who was going to her boyfriend's home one evening, after a school concert.

Other 'Stranger Rape' reviews had unexpected outcomes. For example, in one 1992 case the rapist's DNA profile was developed. However, when it was searched on the National DNA Database (NDNAD) it matched two different men! Enquiries revealed that they were in fact identical twins and, unfortunately for investigators, identical twins always have the same DNA profiles. But nearly twenty years had since elapsed, so would it now be possible to establish which of the brothers had actually committed this rape?

In other cases, the attackers' DNA profiles have been developed, but searches of the NDNAD revealed that they were not recorded thereon. How then might they be identified? The answer (in some cases) lies in a process historically known as Familial DNA Searching. This approach focuses on the past misdeeds of an unknown suspect's blood relative who *is* on the NDNAD, rather than the past misdeeds of the actual offender who isn't. Essex Police is one of a number of forces who have enjoyed some success with this method of investigation.

Occasionally, a 'Cold Case' review will conclude that a particular 'Stranger Rape' allegation was entirely fictitious. Such cases are relatively unusual, but it is just as important to resolve the alleged crime. Not only can a potentially long running and costly investigation be concluded, but innocent parties who may have come under suspicion, perhaps have even been arrested, can be fully exonerated.

But it is not just serious or high profile crimes like murder or 'Stranger Rape' that are referred to the Review Team. Occasionally, it is asked to review other deaths or unusual incidents that have troubled individual families for years, sometimes for decades.

Some sudden or unexpected deaths are clearly murder or manslaughter; but most such deaths occur as a result of natural causes, accidents or suicide. Unfortunately, a few deaths remain unresolved despite the best efforts of the police.

It does not matter that the circumstances of a case strongly indicate suicide; those left behind may still have great difficulty in coming to terms with the death. Many blame themselves for not having seen the signs of a person possibly contemplating suicide and then intervening. But in reality there was probably little they could have done to prevent the suicide.

In some cases relatives or friends refuse to accept that their loved one or friend would even contemplate suicide, let alone actually commit it. And no matter how long ago the death occurred, they feel a duty to try to prove that the death was not suicide, if only to restore the reputation of the deceased. They actively look for evidence to show that the death was in fact accidental, or more unusually, that it was murder made to look like an accident or suicide. Furthermore, it does not help that suicide was once a crime and for some people there is still a stigma attached to it.

An example of such a case is the alleged suicide of Maurice Sams. On the 23rd July 1951, this thirty seven year-old garage owner was found dead in his caravan at Tollesbury, Essex. One end of a hose pipe that had probably dropped off the exhaust pipe of his car was found lying on the ground below it; the other end had been inserted through one of the caravan's windows. Police suspected suicide, but no suicide note was found.

A post mortem examination found that Maurice had died from carbon monoxide poisoning. An Inquest held only days later was told by one of the main witnesses, Clifford Berkelmans, that Maurice had been depressed about various aspects of his life, including his finances; and the Coroner returned a verdict of Suicide. But many years later Maurice's son Nigel acquired documents that revealed a web of intrigue that would not have looked out of place in an Agatha Christie novel!

In particular, they revealed that shortly before her husband's death, Mrs Sams began to suspect that he was having an affair with Ruth Berkelmans, Clifford's wife. He was later to become the main witness. Through solicitors she arranged for private detectives to watch Maurice; and they were doing so during the days leading up to his death. Strangely, neither the police nor the Coroner were ever told about this surveillance operation; nor what the detectives had actually seen, some of which appeared to contradict parts of Mr. Berkelmans' evidence. The documents also revealed that Maurice was not, after all, in any real financial difficulties.

So what other motive may he have had to commit suicide, if any; and just how reliable was the main witness evidence regarding Sams' state of mind just before his death? In short, how safe was the original Suicide verdict? More than fifty years had elapsed since this death, so what might a 'Cold Case' review achieve?

Perhaps one of the most unusual reviews the team conducted followed allegations of child death and child abduction. These were made on behalf of the allegedly 'abducted' child, who was now an eighty three year-old woman! This elderly lady told her son that sometime around 1930, she had been abducted by a local gypsy family to take the place of their baby who had been accidentally smothered and whose body had then been secretly buried. She went on to say that she had been brought up as a member of the 'abductor's' family, but was treated differently from her siblings and never really accepted as one of the family.

Sensing that she was nearing the end of her life, this troubled woman was keen to find her 'real' family so they could at long last be reunited. By then, some eighty years had elapsed since her alleged kidnap; but if this lady was telling the truth, she was still the victim of a historic crime (as were her natural parents) with, perhaps, surviving blood relatives of her birth family. There was also the child who had allegedly been smothered and secretly buried in an unknown grave; and whose death had never been properly investigated. Despite the passage of time, it was important that the allegations were investigated and if possible resolved. And with the help of DNA profiling they were.

Other 'mysteries' include the disappearance of twenty four year-old Robin Perry. He was one of three men who went missing whilst wildfowling on Ministry of Defence (MOD) property at Foulness in 1969. Two bodies were later recovered from the sea, but Robin's has never been found.

In 1969, the MOD site was a Proof and Experimental Establishment; weapons and ammunition were frequently test fired into the estuary off Foulness Island. When the tide turned and the sea mist descended, foreign shipping (including Russian vessels) would anchor off Foulness. Wildfowlers could walk across the mudflats and almost reach them; and presumably the seafarers could almost reach land.

Was the presence of Russian shipping on the night of Robin's disappearance the key to this mystery? It was after all, the height of the 'Cold War'. Spies around the world were allegedly being secretly exchanged; and some members of Robin's family wondered if he had stumbled across one such exchange and had been silenced. They certainly suspected some form of MOD 'cover-up', indeed questions were asked in Parliament by the local MP, Bernard Braine. However, according to the family, no satisfactory answers were ever provided.

But were there other possible explanations for Robin's disappearance and for what some members of the family perceived as an official 'cover up'? Was it perhaps possible that Robin's body had simply washed ashore elsewhere and was amongst the dozens of unidentified bodies and body parts recovered from the seas around the United Kingdom and beyond, during the late 1960's / early 1970's?

Without Robin's fingerprints, dental chart or DNA profile, it would be difficult to eliminate any of those unidentified bodies or body parts from this investigation; difficult, but not impossible.

Finally there are a few cases that I regard as unfinished business. They have been thoroughly investigated and reviewed; and in some cases re-investigated. Suspects have subsequently been identified, but, at the time of writing, there is insufficient evidence to prosecute them.

Unfortunately it is not always possible to identify and then to prosecute all those who committed serious crimes many years ago. However, by carrying out reviews it is often possible to make real progress with an old investigation; and that progress may one day help to finally solve the crime. Arrests and convictions are not, therefore, the only measures of success.

Some of those unsolved cases are also briefly recounted in this book in the certain knowledge that there will be some people who know (or at least strongly suspect) who was responsible for those crimes. The cases include the 1964 abduction, rape and murder of seven year-old Kim Roberts, who disappeared one Sunday evening whilst playing outside her home in the east end of London. Her dead body was found several days later, having been dumped in woods at Purfleet, near Grays, Essex.

For decades the murder remained unsolved. Then, in 2004, an Essex pensioner suddenly broke down and confessed the killing to members of his family. But was he being truthful?

Another brutal unsolved murder occurred in October 1968. Sixty nine year-old Ivy Kemp was subjected to a frenzied knife attack whilst in bed at her home in Laindon. Despite a major investigation, her killer was never caught.

Then, in 2002, as a result of advances in fingerprint technology, a previously unidentified fingerprint recovered from a document found in Ivy's bedroom, was finally identified, prompting a 'Cold Case' review. Enquiries revealed that the man who had left that fingerprint, had since died; but in any event we were able to satisfactorily eliminate him from the enquiry.

But quite unexpectedly, the review identified another individual who was said to have secretly confessed to Ivy's murder soon after the killing, but who had never been properly eliminated from the original murder investigation. But where was he now; and was it too late to bring him to justice?

Similarly, a review of the investigation into the 1975 murder of forty nine year-old Ivy Davies, was also carried out as a result of an alleged historic confession. Ivy, who ran the Orange Tree Café at Westcliff-on-Sea, was battered to death in her home nearby. No one was ever charged with her murder.

But thirty years later, following a fresh appeal for information, someone did come forward. She told us what had allegedly occurred the night Ivy was murdered and named those allegedly involved. However, even if what she was saying was true, the difficulty was always going to be proving it.

Finally, at the time of writing, the unsolved crimes include a series of 'Stranger Rapes' committed in Laindon, Basildon, during the early 1990's. Over a two year period, a number of schoolgirls and other young women were attacked by a man wearing a stocking mask. He threatened them with a Stanley craft knife before carrying out a number of serious sexual assaults. At the time, detectives believed that some, if not all of these attacks, were the work of one man; but he was never caught. Officers' suspicions were later confirmed when DNA profiles of the women's attacker proved beyond doubt that some of those assaults had indeed been committed by the same man.

This book, whilst not purporting to represent the views of Essex Police (or even of other members of the Review Team) provides an insight into their day-to-day work and lives of the victims of some of the most serious crimes committed in Essex during the past few decades; and of their families. Similarly, it provides an insight into the lives of some of those who committed those crimes.

It describes the original crimes and other serious incidents, the resulting investigations and finally, the more recent work of the Major Crime Review and Investigation Teams.

Where suspects have been interviewed but not charged, yet have still been named by the media, I have not provided their full names in this book. Those prosecuted and convicted have been named.

The work carried out by Essex Police has meant that at least some of the victims detailed within this book have, in every sense of the words, been finally laid to rest.

Some people will read this book with interest; hopefully a few will now be dreading the knock on the door which will come on that day when their own past finally catches up with them. Of course, they always have the option of pre-empting that visit by going to the police and facing up to their crimes, some of which were committed many years ago when they were different people leading totally different lives.

Hopefully, others will read this book and find the courage to tell the police what they know about a particular unsolved murder or other serious crime. This will always be in confidence and if necessary can be done anonymously via Crimestoppers on 0800 555 111.

CHAPTER 2
THE RAPE AND MURDER OF NORAH TROTT

The evening following Guy Fawkes Night is always dark, usually dank and somehow depressing. Smoke still hangs in the air, distilling the excitement of a thousand children. The evening of Monday 6th November 1978 was no different. And when sixty three year-old Norah Margaret Trott left home she could have no idea that she was taking a short walk to a sudden, undignified and extremely violent death.

Why would she suspect this? After all, Norah lived in the small market town of Rochford, still one of the safest places in the country in which to live and to work. True, Rochford is only a few miles from the bustling urban sprawl that is Southend-on-Sea; but it is off the main routes to and from London (the A127 and A13) and unless you did live or work there, it is not a town one would normally go to without a reason.

But that reason might be to experience its history. Rochford is one of the oldest and most historic towns in Essex; in fact, objects recovered locally have been traced back to the Stone Age. In all probability, the settlement was originally established because it is close to the sea, allowing its early inhabitants to fish and to hunt for their food. However, its location also made it vulnerable to attack by other nations, including the continental Beaker-folk (so called because they insisted on burying their beakers with them, for the next life), the Romans, Picts, Scots, Saxons and Danes.

Centuries later, it became the haunt of King Henry VIII and his 'Lady Anne (Boleyn) of Rochford'. She lived in the Manor of Rochford which was mentioned in the Doomsday Book in 1086. Her former home, Rochford Hall, still stands and together with the surrounding land now forms the Rochford Hundred Golf Club.

Rochford's main thoroughfares converge at a crossroad in the town centre. South Street (when travelling from the Southend-on-Sea direction) leads into North Street, now part of the one-way system.

The junction is transected by East Street, which (when travelling from the Stambridge direction) crosses into West Street; both are now one-way streets. West Street is also the home of the long established market place which still opens every Tuesday morning.

The town had (and still has) many alehouses, one of which was the Old Ship Inn, then located in North Street. At one time, iron rings were affixed to the outside wall so that travelling fairground workers could tether their performing bears, whilst they themselves popped inside for a drink! The building itself still stands, although at the time of writing it is no longer used as a public house.

Old Ship Lane is immediately to the right of what was the Old Ship Inn. This one way street leads from East Street back into North Street. Part way up Old Ship Lane, on the right hand side (when travelling from North Street) there once stood a newer public house, the appropriately named New Ship Inn. Again, the building itself remains, but it is no longer used as a public house.

Further up the lane and just before it meets East Street, the road bends to the right. On the left hand apex of this bend, there was once a short driveway that led to a block of three lock-up garages owned by Hawkwell Parish Council. These have long since been demolished and a health centre now occupies the site.

The garage on the left hand side of the block was rented by a local man who was interested in vintage cars. That garage was seldom accessed, so a Volvo car belonging to another local resident was often parked in front of it. The middle garage was rented by Norah Trott and housed her Morris 1100 saloon car registration number WAJ 182J. The garage to the right was rented by the local council.

Norah was a well-liked and much respected member of the local community. She was said by many to be attractive and to look much younger than her years. Norah had once been married to Ronald Trott, a barrister who later became a judge; but they divorced in 1960.

Nevertheless, both had remained on good terms with each other and when Ronald later re-married, Norah became like an aunt to the two children of his second wife. Norah's only other living relative was her sister Teresa (known as Tessa) who lived in nearby Hawkwell.

Norah was a founder member and Secretary of the Rochford Chamber of Trade. She enjoyed sailing, dining out and going to the theatre. Norah was also an animal lover, feeding and caring for stray cats in the area. If they became ill or injured, she would take them to the local vet for treatment, all at her own expense.

Norah lived alone in the flat above her ladies clothing shop, 'Felicity Jane', 7 – 9 North Street, Rochford. The shop (and therefore her flat) faced directly onto Old Ship Lane, so Norah had only to walk eighty or so yards from the flat in order to reach her garage.

Being November, darkness had already descended when Norah left home. However, she was not worried about being on her own. The roads were well illuminated by street lamps and the light exuding from both the Old and New Ship public houses; and there were quite a few people about. Nevertheless, few women feel entirely safe when walking alone at night, especially through the back streets. Norah would certainly feel a little happier once she was safely inside her car. But it was not to be.

Norah is believed to have left home sometime after seven o'clock that evening. Her intention was to visit a long-standing friend, Frank Prime, who lived in Southend-on-Sea. Prime had been a little unwell and Norah had promised to visit him that evening taking with her some 'creature comforts', including newspapers, magazines, chocolate and fruit juice.

Norah hurried up Old Ship Lane, in all probability completely unaware of the young man observing her every movement. She walked onto the driveway leading to her garage, took the garage key from her handbag, then unlocked and removed the padlock.

The young man silently crept forward; Norah was now within his grasp.

His first blow knocked Norah almost senseless; blood splattered across the garage doors and door frame and she fell to the ground. Norah tried to call out for help, but the attacker stamped on her throat crushing her voice box. Now, barely conscious, he dragged her to a narrow overgrown alleyway between the left hand side garage and the brick-built back garden wall of the Old Ship Pubic House. There he stripped Norah of her clothing, including her boots, before violently raping her.

Then, as silently as he had arrived, the attacker disappeared into the night, taking with him Norah's shopping bag and other items of personal property. Norah died shortly after.

When Norah failed to arrive at his home, Frank Prime became a little concerned. He telephoned Norah's flat, but got no reply. He then called Teresa, but she told him she had neither seen nor spoken to her sister that evening. Another close friend of Norah's, Alan Cater, was also contacted. He lived locally and had a key to Norah's flat; but Cater had not seen or spoken to Norah that evening.

Further attempts were made to locate Norah, but without success. Consequently, sometime after midnight (Tuesday 7.11.1978) Cater went to Norah's flat. On finding no one there, he went to Norah's garage. He found the garage doors slightly open and Norah's car still inside. Looking around, he saw her handbag laying on the ground by the parked Volvo, but there was no sign of Norah herself.

Shortly before 1am Cater telephoned the police and in due course police constables Matthews and Kirby attended. They noted that the engine of Norah's car was cold and also saw her handbag on the ground. The officers then went to Norah's flat, but on finding it empty they returned to the garage area. As they searched the area more closely, the officers saw spots of blood on the frame to the right of the garage door and the padlock lying on the ground. It appeared to them that Norah may have been attacked as she was opening the garage doors.

The immediate area was again searched and within minutes the officers found Norah's dead body lying in the overgrown alleyway. Norah's blue peaked cap, two belts, a glove and bracelet had been discarded by her body. The other glove, together with her broken glasses, was found by the garage door. The rest of Norah's clothing including her coat, blouse, bra, skirt, slip and two cardigans, had been placed, quite tidily, in the boot of her car.

A major investigation was immediately launched with Detective Inspector (later Superintendent) Ken Smith of Southend-on-Sea CID appointed as the Officer in Charge. At the time this was the largest murder investigation ever undertaken by the then Essex and Southend-on-Sea Joint Constabulary (now Essex Police); and for the first time in a murder investigation, police used what was then described as 'audio visual equipment' i.e. video cameras. They were also to later use hypnotist Dr David Wexman to obtain a detailed description and an artist's impression of the main suspect.

The local police surgeon, Dr Bendkowski (fondly known as 'Dr Ben'), attended the crime scene around 2.30am and formally certified life extinct. Dr Ben estimated that death had probably occurred between two and a half and six hours earlier, i.e. between 8.30pm and midnight.

In fact, establishing the time of death is not as easy as was once believed. Rectal and ambient temperatures were usually taken soon after the discovery of a body in the belief that the rate at which the body had since cooled may give an indication of how long that person had been dead. Doctors then used a rather complicated formula to reach their conclusions. This was later explained to me, but I am not sure I ended up any the wiser!

Apparently, the starting point of their calculation was that the normal temperature of a living human body is 37 degrees centigrade. By subtracting the rectal temperature reading from that figure and dividing the results by 1.5 the doctor would arrive at a certain figure.

This could then be compared with another 'known' fact i.e. that after 18 to 24 hours the temperature of the corpse will be the same as the ambient temperature around it. By taking regular rectal readings, the doctor could work out the time that the body last had a temperature of 37 degrees, therefore, the time when the body was alive.

Easy when you know how!

But there have always been additional factors that can influence the results, for example, the location e.g. whether it is inside a building or outdoors and exposed to the elements, the body type, the amount of clothing worn by the deceased, etc. (I recall attending the post mortem of a tramp; we had to remove six layers of clothing from her before the examination could begin!)

It also used to be thought that an examination of the stomach contents could assist in estimating the time of death. If the time of the last meal was known, the time of death might be estimated by the degree of digestion that had since taken place. Unfortunately, the rate of digestion can vary significantly from person to person, consequently this method could not always be relied upon. Having said that, there have recently been significant advances in this area of pathology.

Interestingly, when poisoning was a more common cause of death, it often used to be said (of the victim) that he or she had died after their last meal; but of course, we all die after our last meal!

Once a body dies the process of decomposition begins and this may give further clues as to how long a body has been dead. Rigor Mortis (the stiffening of muscles after death) begins immediately and on average takes about twelve hours to complete. Hypostasis (post-mortem staining) will usually develop within five hours of death; and within days the skin colour and texture will also change.

If the body has been buried, the surrounding conditions will also affect it. For example, if the conditions are dry the body may become mummified.

Furthermore, if the body has been infected by insects, an entomologist may be able to identify the insects and the stage of growth they have reached. From that, the expert can then calculate the earliest date the eggs could have been laid on the body, therefore, the date when the deceased died; or at least, the date when the body may have been deposited where it was found.

There may also be other clues on or around the body that provide further indications of when death may have occurred, such as newspapers or letters piling up in a hallway, or perhaps a broken wristwatch.

Over time I found that some pathologists were becoming more and more reluctant to commit themselves to a time of death. I once asked a pathologist examining a body to give me an approximate time of death. He asked when the deceased was last seen alive. '8 o'clock last night.' I replied.

'And when was he found dead?'

'6 o'clock this morning.'

'In that case, I think he died between 8 o'clock last night and six this morning!'

100% accurate; but not much help!

A post mortem examination of Norah Trott's body was subsequently carried out by the eminent Home Office Pathologist, Professor James Cameron. A pathologist is a scientist who studies the causes of diseases and how they affect people and the causes of death, by performing post mortem examinations. Post Mortems are often referred to as 'autopsies'. The word is taken from the Latin root 'seeing with one's own eyes.'

For reasons that will shortly be explained, when conducting post mortem examinations where there are no suspicious circumstances, pathologists generally follow routine procedures that have been developed over time.

But where a suspicious death is thought to have occurred, a *forensic* post mortem will be required and this can only be carried out by a Home Office (HO) approved forensic pathologist. HO Pathologists will have undergone further medico / legal training for a number of important reasons.

Firstly, where criminal proceedings could result from an unnatural death, such as murder, the suspect is entitled to have a second post mortem undertaken on his or her behalf, i.e. one independent of the State. Consequently, the HO Pathologist must maintain a detailed record of the first autopsy. This will require the taking of notes, drawing sketches, obtaining video and photographic evidence, the preservation of tissue, organs and injury sites, etc.

The 'defence' pathologist (or independent pathologist if no one has been charged) conducting the second autopsy must also maintain detailed records of his / her work because if the two pathologists fail to agree on any significant points, a third post mortem may be required. One can only imagine the difficulties faced by the third pathologist tasked with examining a body that is now in a significantly different condition to when it was examined by the first pathologist.

Secondly, important forensic evidence may be found on the body and on any clothing the deceased was wearing when killed. Consequently, all examinations must be carried out in a way that secures and preserves that evidence. In fact, it is not unusual for pathologists and other forensic experts to visit a dead body in-situ and advise on how the body is to be removed from the crime scene to the mortuary. Their attendance can also assist a reconstruction of the events leading to the death.

Nowadays the head and hands are normally bagged and the body wrapped and removed in a 'body bag'. This prevents the loss of any forensic evidence during transportation. I recall one particular case where a bullet was subsequently found in a body bag, having exited from the body during transportation. It could so easily have been lost

Another difference between a general pathologist and a forensic pathologist is that a general pathologist dealing with a natural death may have an idea of the possible cause of death at the outset and can focus on the relevant parts of the body. For example, if a person with a history of heart failure suddenly dies of a suspected heart attack, the pathologist can initially focus on an examination of the heart.

But a forensic pathologist cannot simply focus on what may be an obvious cause of death. S/he must rule out any other possible causes or contributory factors, including accident, suicide and natural causes. The pathologist must also establish the level of alcohol in the blood, identify and quantify any drugs or poisons ingested. In short, HO Pathologists must be open-minded and then prepared to share their findings and conclusions.

Amongst other things, Professor Cameron found that Norah had sustained serious head injuries including a compound fracture of the nose, a fractured cheekbone, a fractured palate and, as previously stated, a crushed voice box. One of Norah's teeth had also been knocked out and was found still lodged in her throat. The cause of death was given as asphyxia due to the inhalation of blood.

Norah had also been raped and buggered around the time of her death. Semen was recovered from internal swabs and from Norah's skirt. However, this was likely to be of limited use as it was well before the science of DNA had become available to investigators. But scientists still knew that it might at least identify the attacker's blood group if he was a 'Secretor'. At that time more that 80% of the world's population were 'Secretors', that is to say their blood cells were also present in other body fluids like saliva or semen. However, at that time, there were nearly 290 different blood types, all developed from four main groupings, i.e.:

- Group 'A' (40% of the world's population)
- Group 'AB' - a variant of Group 'A' (5% of the world's population)
- Group 'B' (15% of the world's population), and finally,
- Group 'O' (40% of the world's population).

Tests on the semen recovered from the internal swabs revealed that the attacker was indeed a 'Secretor' and that his blood group was 'A', therefore 40% of the world's population. Furthermore, tests carried out on the semen found on Norah's skirt identified additional variants that only occurred in 7% of the population; but this was still a significant number of men.

But whilst the blood group alone could not be used to positively identify the person responsible, it could be used to eliminate from the enquiry any suspects who had a different blood group to the killer.

Numerous fingerprints were recovered from the crime scene, but one by one they were matched to people who had legitimate access to the garage, the garage area and Norah's car.

Except for one fingerprint.

This was found on a plastic carrier bag in the boot of Norah's car, next to her clothing. Unfortunately, that fingerprint impression was of such poor quality that fingerprint experts could not determine which finger, or even which hand, had left the mark. In any event, Detective Inspector Smith was doubtful that the fingerprint had been left by the killer; and he was later to be proved right.

A Murder Incident Office was set up at the local police station and as the murder predated computerisation, all statements, reports and other records were hand written and / or typed, in triplicate. A police incident caravan was also parked near the crime scene and remained there for the first two weeks of the investigation.

Over twenty detectives were drafted in to form an Outside Enquiries Team. Their first priority was to establish exactly who had been in the area at the relevant time so as to identify possible witnesses and suspects. All local public houses were visited by detectives. Staff and customers were interviewed in an attempt to identify every person who had been in or around the Rochford town centre on the night of Norah's murder.

Those and other enquiries quickly enabled detectives to construct the sequence of events that had occurred during the period immediately before, during and after Norah's murder.

The last confirmed sighting of Norah Trott was around 6pm on the night she was murdered. A witness who knew her personally, saw Norah standing in the doorway of her shop.

This witness also saw a young faired haired man standing outside the Old Ship Public House. He was looking at Norah and she was looking back at him.

Between 5.50pm and 6.05pm, there were further sightings of a slim, fair haired man, in the area, variously described as being in his late teens to mid-twenties. He was observed sitting, and at other times standing, on the low wall surrounding the small car park to the right hand side of the New Ship Public House (when facing the front of the building). In fact, he was sitting directly opposite the garages, one of which housed Norah's car.

Sometime between 7pm and 7.30pm, Norah telephoned one of her part-time employees to discuss duties, so police knew that Norah was still alive then.

Enquiries also revealed that around 7.45pm, two local boys had been seen in the very garage area where the murder was committed. They were hanging around the Volvo parked therein. When subsequently traced and interviewed, they told police they had seen nothing untoward in that garage area. If true, this suggested that the attack had not occurred by then.

They told detectives they had seen a bonfire still burning in the rear garden of the Old Ship Public House, the remnants of a private party organised by the landlord, Henry Knowles. The boys said they had spoken to the landlord's mother-in-law, Doris Gilder, but after finding out that there would be no more fireworks that night, the boys went home. Doris remained in the back garden, alone.

When interviewed Doris said that shortly after 8.05pm, she heard a rustling noise behind the back wall which separated the rear garden from the garage block. Suddenly, a young man's head popped up from behind that wall. Alarmed by this, Doris went back inside the pub and fetched her husband, Alfred. He came out and challenged the young man who was still behind the wall, coming to within three feet of him.

The young man then said, 'I've got a woman here.'

Thinking they had disturbed a courting couple, the Gilders went back into the public house. Doris was later to describe this man as white, nineteen to twenty one years-of-age, clean shaven with long brown or blonde hair. Mr and Mrs Gilder later helped the police to compile photo-fits and artist's impressions of the 'baby faced' suspect. The final artist impression was said to be a very good likeness of him.

Around the same time as the Gilders' sighting of the young man, a young couple out with their baby and Alsatian dog, walked up Old Ship Lane towards their home in nearby East Street. They later recalled that the dog had growled and pulled towards the garage area just as they were passing. The couple continued walking home and arrived there around 8.20pm.

As they were about to enter their house, a man carrying a cream or off-white bag jogged past them. He ran from the direction of Old Ship Lane, along East Street, towards Stambridge. Shortly after, a woman who lived in nearby Greenways also saw a man carrying a shopping bag. He was jogging down the middle of her road and disappeared further along that road where two alleyways meet. One alleyway leads into Weir Pond Road near its junction with East Street and the other leads into Oast Way.

However, the next and most important sighting of the suspect that evening, occurred shortly after the Greenways report, in Oast Way itself. This suggested that the man had run through the alleyway from Greenways into Oast Way. Two local boys, Christopher and Philip, were out on their bicycles and saw a young man acting suspiciously outside the house where one of the boys then lived.

The man appeared to be carrying something close to his chest and when he walked off they decided to follow him. They watched as he went into the cul-de-sac at the far end of Oast Way, where he put something into a dustbin bag outside one of the houses. The man then retraced his steps back out of the cul-de-sac before running into an alleyway that led from Oast Way back into North Street.

The boys followed him through the alleyway and back towards the town centre. Finally, they watched him turn left into East Street; by then he was about one hundred yards from the murder scene. When the man disappeared into East Street, Philip was only twenty five yards behind him. But as Philip cycled round the corner, he saw a police minivan stationary outside the local off-licence. Another police mini was driving towards him, the driver of which sounded his horn at Philip, who was riding his bicycle the wrong way up the one-way street! The boy immediately alighted from his bicycle, but by then he had lost sight of the man he had been following.

At the time, some officers thought that as the suspect's route had taken him through back roads and alleyways, he must have had some local knowledge. But did he live locally or had he just been running blindly, not knowing where exactly he was going? Why else would he have ended up almost back at the crime scene?

Both boys returned to the cul-de-sac in Oast Way and from the dustbin bag the man had been touching, they retrieved a straw shopping bag containing various items. They included two newspapers, two magazines, two bottles of fruit juice, a jar of stewed apples and a bar of chocolate.

They took the bag to Philip's home, but on arrival his mother noticed what appeared to be blood-staining on the bag. She told them to take it to Rochford Police Station which they did, but it was closed so they dialled '999'.

The officer who responded to their '999' call was constable Stuart Bines. They told him what they had seen and handed the bag over.

PC Bines also went to the cul-de-sac at the end of Oast Way and on looking around found a pair of blood-stained nail scissors laying on a nearby drive. The scissors were later identified by her sister, as belonging to Norah Trott. PC Bines later recalled that he had initially thought that the shopping bag had been stolen from a car and that the thief had cut himself in the process of stealing from it. PC Bines then tried to find the car, but without success. The bag itself contained no identifiable property and as Norah had not yet been reported missing, the officer had no idea who the bag and its contents might belong to. It was, therefore, booked in as 'found property'.

The following day the police (having found Norah's body during the night) began a thorough search of the town centre. They were looking for Norah's missing clothing and any other personal property or possible murder weapon. As a result of that search, Norah's upper denture, which was wrapped in her knickers, together with her two purses, were found on waste ground adjacent to the off-licence in East Street.

It is believed that when the suspect turned into East Street, he had also seen the police vehicles and had panicked. In all probability he had run across the waste ground, abandoning the property as he went. Perhaps significantly, no money appeared to have been stolen from either of the purses.

The straw bag was later shown to the couple who had been out with their baby and dog; one of them identified it as the bag the suspect had been carrying as he ran past them.

Two hundred police officers from around the county were drafted into Rochford the weekend following the murder. Their main task was to undertake house-to-house enquiries. Initially, those enquiries centred on Rochford itself, but during the next few weeks and months enquiries radiated out to surrounding villages and hamlets.

Full descriptions and other personal details were required of every male of between ten and forty years of age, who was interviewed. They were asked to provide full details of their movements on the night in question, plus the names and contact details of anyone who could verify their movements.

Polaroid photographs were also taken of many of those interviewed. These were later made into photograph albums which were then shown to important witnesses, but no identifications were made. During this process a number of possible suspects were identified, most of whom voluntarily provided blood and / or saliva samples, all to no avail.

One might perhaps be forgiven for thinking that there would not have been too many young men in or around a small town like Rochford on a Monday evening. Unfortunately, there were literally hundreds! Rochford Hospital was just off the town centre and their services also included mental health and maternity units. Husbands and other relatives visited the maternity unit all hours of the day and night. Other local premises included the dozen or so public houses, the popular Rocheway Youth Centre and two council-run boy's hostels, one in Market Square and the other in Southend Road.

The town was also popular with soldiers from Shoebury Garrison and sailors from ships visiting the flour mill at Stambridge and the Baltic Timber Wharf at nearby Wallasea. Prison absconders, army deserters and local sex offenders were also traced and interviewed, but the trail went cold.

In February 1979, detectives attended Norah's funeral at St Teresa's Roman Catholic Church in Rochford, hoping to find more leads, again to no avail.

The investigation slowly wound down, albeit that two local detectives maintained a 'watching brief', following up any new lines of enquiry. By this time, 4,000 households had been visited and 11,000 individuals spoken to. Eight hundred statements had been taken, nine hundred enquiries completed and seventy voluntary blood samples obtained. But detectives seemed to be no nearer to catching the killer.

During most long-running murder investigations, certain individuals are identified as good suspects, either by their own family or friends / associates; or by police officers who have previously come into contact with them. This investigation was no different, but none of the suspects could be connected to the murder.

At one stage Norah's friend Alan Cater also became a suspect after detectives found a blood stained lump of wood in his car. Fortunately for him, this turned out to be rabbit's blood!

However, one particular individual did become a prime suspect and in some officers' eyes, remained so for many years. His name was Hugh Townsend. He was a young, vulnerable adult with learning difficulties and his father was the local veterinary surgeon used by Norah. Unfortunately for Hugh, he fitted the suspect's description and even looked like the suspect's photo-fits and artist's impressions. Worse still, he lived less than fifty yards from Norah's garage.

Enquiries revealed that on the evening of the murder, he had left home, alone, to visit his grandmother who lived nearby. Afterwards he popped into the same off-licence in East Street that the killer had later passed by. He, therefore, had no real alibi for the actual time of the murder. Hugh was arrested on suspicion of murder and a blood sample was taken from him. It did not match the suspect's blood group, so he was released without charge. However, Townsend repeatedly came to detectives' attention. One day during the summer of 1980, Doris Gilder saw the suspect again, this time as he was crossing North Street into Old Ship Lane. Unfortunately she then lost sight of him.

Then, in March 1981, she saw him again, this time as they were both travelling on a bus from Southend-on-Sea to Rochford. On reaching the Rochford town centre, he got off the bus and walked across the road into Old Ship Lane. Doris followed him to veterinary surgery in East Street and the police were informed. They quickly identified the suspect as Hugh Townsend and later carried out a street identification outside the training centre he attended. Doris formally identified him as the young man she had seen in the alleyway where Norah's body had later been found; also on the two subsequent occasions. But once again, Townsend was forensically eliminated from this crime.

Finally, in 1993, further information was received by police suggesting that Hugh may hold important information relating to Norah Trott's murder. He was arrested on an unrelated matter, but later released without charge.

However, whilst in custody he was again questioned about the murder of Norah Trott, but continued to deny any knowledge of, or involvement in, the murder. Once again, was forensically eliminated from the investigation.

No evidence was ever found to link Hugh Townsend to the murder and I am satisfied that he was not involved in the actual attack. But he still could have been the man seen by the Gilders that night. I believe it is possible that whilst out that night, Hugh may have seen or heard something going on near the garages and on investigating 'stumbled' across Norah's body. Then, when challenged by Doris Gilder and her husband he said, 'I've got a woman here'.

That would have been an understandable response from a person with his learning difficulties; it was not necessarily evidence of any involvement in the murder itself. If indeed this is what happened, he could have told the police when they arrested him. But by then he may have been too frightened to admit to *anything* that might directly connect him to the murder, a position he had to maintain thereafter.

On a positive note, this was a case where forensic science eliminated a suspect against whom there had clearly been some evidence, albeit identification and circumstantial evidence. But on the negative side, extensive media reporting of the murder undoubtedly contributed to a climate of fear within some local communities.

One local rumour that had spread as far as Basildon, Essex, was that a woman had returned to her car to find a man dressed in women's clothing, sitting inside it. He had then run off and when the car was searched, an axe was allegedly found on the back seat. Interestingly, this 'Urban Myth', and variations thereof, continues to be circulated across the United Kingdom and probably beyond.

One of the current 'Urban Myths' concerns someone who allegedly performed an act of kindness towards a Muslim, who was so grateful that he warned the 'good Samaritan', not to use the underground system the next day. The inference was that he knew about a planned terrorist attack on London.

But, like all 'Urban Myths', it is never possible to actually track down the would-be victim or witness. He or she is always an un-named or unknown 'friend of a friend'. Nevertheless, those hearing the story feel almost a duty to warn their friends and others, including the police.

And so it goes on .....

The murder investigation eventually came to a standstill and all the papers and other case material were archived pending any new information or other developments. At that time, detectives were not at all confident that the Norah Trott murder would ever be solved; 'Cold Case' Reviews had never even been heard of.

Rather frustratingly for them, it seemed that Norah's killer was going to get away with murder.

CHAPTER 3
THE REVIEW OF THE NORAH TROTT MURDER

The Essex Police Major Crime Review Team was set up in August 2003, the founder members being the author and ex-Detective Chief Inspector Peter Hamilton. The main aim was for us to review unsolved major crimes which were then being actively investigated. But Chief Officers were also keen that we should begin reviewing some of Essex Police's unsolved 'Cold Cases'. The murder of Norah Trott was chosen as the first 'Cold Case' murder review. I was to be the lead reviewer since Peter was leading on a separate case.

The twenty fifth anniversary of Norah's murder was approaching and fresh information about the murder had just been received. A woman contacted the police claiming that some days before the murder she had also been attacked by a man in Rochford, but had managed to fight him off with the help of two members of the public. She had not previously reported this attack to the police. The woman also told police that she used to wear a leather coat similar to one often worn by Norah.

Could the attack upon her have been a case of mistaken identity; was Norah the intended victim that day?

Quite separately, an anonymous letter about the murderer had also been received by the police. In it, the author said that the killer was from Ilford and drove a white or cream car. The man was said to have been a regular customer at the Old Ship Public House and to have often pestered blonde women to join him for a drink; and would become angry if they refused. The letter was forensically examined for any fingerprints or other evidence that might identify the author, but nothing useful was found.

In fact, neither lines of enquiry took the case forward, but they and the forthcoming anniversary of the murder, provided the 'springboard' for a fresh media appeal which was subsequently made.

Norah's sister Teresa had since died, but as a matter of courtesy I spoke to Norah's ex-husband Ronald.

This was primarily to make him aware of the review and to prepare him for the media attention that this review would undoubtedly attract. He was both surprised and delighted to learn that the police were reviewing the case and said that he would continue to co-operate with us. Despite this, I think he privately doubted that Norah's killer would ever be caught; but then again, we were also far from certain that he would be.

Nevertheless, it was important to present a positive attitude and at a specially convened press conference I pointed out that as the killer was between nineteen and twenty five years of age at the time of Norah's murder, he would not now be too old to serve a life sentence. (But we would have to catch him first!) The media appeal resulted in further calls from the public suggesting more names of possible suspects. These would all be followed up.

The twenty fifth anniversary of Norah Trott's murder arrived on the 6th November 2003. That evening I parked my car in the car park overlooking the original crime scene. My intention was to see what it might have looked like on the night of the murder. However, in the back of my mind was the knowledge that a criminal will sometimes return to the scene of their crime in a bizarre attempt to re-live it. The recent publicity might tempt Norah's killer to do likewise.

But what would I do if he did? After all, I was no longer a police officer, albeit that I was a member of Essex Police Support Staff. I decided to cross that bridge in the unlikely event that he did show up. I was not taking much of a risk as I had a mobile phone with me. Also, my son Simon was one of the police officers patrolling Rochford that night; he knew what I was up to.

Half an hour went by and then suddenly (and quite spookily) I heard the footsteps of a woman walking quickly in my direction up Old Ship Lane. But just as suddenly, the footsteps stopped. On investigating, I found there was a small door at the back of the New Ship Public House and concluded that she must have gone in there; at least, I hoped she had!

The rest of the evening was uneventful, but from time to time my mind went back to the violent attack on this kindly woman; hopefully she was unconscious for most of it.

I quietly promised that we would do all we could to catch her killer.

Having launched the review, the next task was to recover all the original documents and other case material that had been archived within some thirty storage boxes. These were collected from our Central Property Store and delivered to an office at Rayleigh Police Station, from where this review would be conducted.

I should, perhaps, point out that the way we go about our work actually bears little resemblance to that depicted in popular BBC TV dramas like 'New Tricks' or 'Waking The Dead'. We do not, at least on a daily basis, liaise with detectives, pathologists and forensic scientists; nor are we out there interviewing witnesses and suspects. Our cases also take more than a week or so to resolve!

But to be fair, a drama that focussed on three or four retired detectives sitting in front of computers, studying archived reports, statements and exhibits, etc., would not make very entertaining television. Nevertheless, our work is very interesting and when it results in the unmasking of a murder or rapist who thought they had escaped punishment for their crimes, it is just as exciting and very satisfying.

During the first few days of the review I spoke to a number of serving and retired officers who had been involved in the original investigation, but no fresh information was obtained.

The next three months were spent 'ploughing' through the case material, making copious notes during the process and discussing my findings and theories with Peter Hamilton. The now dilapidated card index systems that had once formed the backbone of the original Incident Office, had to be sorted and re-arranged so that every card was back in subject, alphabetical and numerical order. In effect, the original Incident Office records had to be physically reconstructed.

Nowadays all this information is routinely computerised and can be researched and sorted at the touch of a button.

But it would have taken months of work by a HOLMES (Home Office Large Major Enquiry System) team to put all this archived information onto a computer database before it could be researched

This would have delayed the review and would have been a waste of scarce resources if the review was unsuccessful in identifying the killer. Consequently, I had to read every original statement, police officer's report and all other documents. Though this was time consuming it had to be done as I needed to know the case 'inside out' and to be able to easily research the case material as the review progressed.

If, for example, a statement referred to the driver of a red car acting suspiciously at a particular location, I had to be in a position to identify all the red cars that came into the original enquiry, plus their owners and drivers. This was so those people could be further researched, especially any whose names had already come up more than once during the investigation. It is so often the case that the name of the killer is to be found amongst the mountain of paperwork or computer data generated during any murder investigation.

The Yorkshire Ripper murder investigation is a case in point. Between 1975 and 1980, Peter Sutcliffe was routinely interviewed by police officers on at least nine occasions. Unfortunately, those officers were from a number of different police forces, investigating different murders and following up separate lines of enquiry. But between them, they had gathered important and detailed information about Sutcliff, his movements and the vehicles he drove.

At that time, detectives also knew quite a lot about the Yorkshire Ripper. They knew, for example, that he wore Wellington boots sized 7.5 or 8; that he had visited Leeds, Bradford, Halifax, Manchester and Huddersfield and that he owned or used a car fitted with an Avon 'Super Safety' tyre and an India 'Autoway' tyre.

The information gathered about Peter Sutcliffe also matched what was known about the Yorkshire Ripper, but, with the possible exception of one officer, no one made the links or recognised Sutcliffe's potential importance to the investigations.

His was just one amongst thousands of names recorded during this mammoth investigation, albeit that it had come up several times.

In the end it was a routine stop-check by uniformed officers that finally led to Sutcliffe's arrest, rather than all the previous years of detective work.

I, therefore, knew that the name of Norah's killer was very likely to be on one or more of the archived documents; but which one?

Many of the original exhibits were also re-examined using modern fingerprint development techniques. In particular, we were looking for fingerprints that had not previously been found. This work resulted in further fingerprints being developed, but rather disappointingly, all were subsequently linked to innocent parties.

The exhibits had also to be reviewed to see if any recent advances in forensic science, such as DNA, might assist. In fact our first and perhaps most important discovery was that a partial DNA profile of the attacker had once been developed. It had been searched on the National DNA Database, but having come back 'no trace' the enquiry was not pursued.

Our next important discovery was that the unidentified fingerprint recovered from a plastic shopping bag in the boot of Norah Trott's car, had still not been identified. Since 1978, there had been considerable advances in technology so that even poor quality fingerprint impressions could now be searched on the National Automated Fingerprint Identification System (NAFIS).

This unidentified fingerprint was recovered from archived fingerprint records and searched on the national database. It immediately matched the fingerprints of a petty criminal, 'Peter Brown' (not his real name). 'Peter's' background and current whereabouts were urgently enquired into, but the results of those enquiries were somewhat perplexing. According to police records and other information available to them, 'Peter' had never been to Essex and he had certainly not featured in the original investigation.

'Peter' seemed to have spent most of his life in London and around the southern counties, including Sussex. He was now living and working on a remote farm in Wales. 'Peter' had no previous convictions for violence or sex offences and his DNA profile was not on the National DNA Database.

Detectives went to Wales where 'Peter' was interviewed. He confirmed that he had never been to Essex and said he did not know Norah Trott. A voluntary DNA sample was obtained from him and in due course, his DNA profile was developed. It was compared with the killer's part DNA profile and did not match.

So how had his fingerprints ended up on a plastic bag in the boot of Norah's car? One possible explanation is that as 'Peter' had frequented the same parts of Sussex that Norah had often visited, they may have unknowingly come into contact with each other. Norah's hairdresser, for example, had moved from Essex to Burgess Hill and her dentist had moved to Horley, both in Sussex. Norah had regularly visited them; consequently, it was possible that at some stage 'Peter' had touched the bag whilst out shopping, or perhaps had even served and given the bag to Norah. In any event, there was no other evidence linking 'Peter' to the crime scene and, more importantly, he was forensically eliminated from the attack via his DNA.

We then turned out attention back to the original part DNA profile and discovered that there were real problems with it. Firstly, it was a part mixed profile, that is to say it was not a full DNA profile and contained the DNA of more than one person. Secondly, as it was a part mixed profile it could not be permanently loaded onto the National DNA Database (NDNAD). It could not, therefore, be automatically searched as and when new profiles were added to the database.

As previously stated, a speculative search of the NDNAD had once been carried out, but the killer's profile did not match any individual then on the database. However, it had not been checked since that original search, so this was done as a matter of urgency. Unfortunately, it still came back 'no trace'.

Enquiries also revealed that both the police and the Forensic Science Service still had other biological material relating to the Norah Trott murder.

That material included a number of blood-stained items, plus the tooth recovered from her throat during the original post mortem examination. From these items it was possible to develop Norah's own DNA profile.

That profile was then removed from the part mixed DNA profile and finally gave us a part DNA profile of the killer himself. Again, this was searched on the NDNAD, but still no match was found. Being a part profile, it still could not be loaded onto the NDNAD, but this time arrangements were made for the profile to be routinely checked each month as more and more suspects' DNA profiles were loaded thereon. One day it might produce a match.

Next, we had to consider whether or not Hugh Townsend had been wrongly eliminated. Could there have been mix up of samples at the Forensic Science Laboratory? I arranged for the movements and storage of all samples relating to Norah's murder to be reviewed and once this had been done there was no doubting that the part DNA profile that had been developed, originated from Norah's killer; and it definitely did not match Hugh's Townsend's DNA profile.

Meanwhile, as the review progressed, names of other young men who had come into the original investigation were collated and researched. It was quickly established that at least thirty of them had not been satisfactorily alibied for the night of the murder. Most had claimed they were with their wives or girlfriends; but loyal partners do not always tell the truth, especially if they cannot actually remember what their partner was doing on the night in question. In any event, they normally do not believe their man to be capable of such a crime. The killer could, therefore, be a man thought to have previously been alibied, but who had not actually been home that night or who had popped out for a while.

There were also a number of men who were unknown to police in 1978, but had since become violent criminals and / or sex offenders. They had not been closely looked at in 1978 because of their good character; but they would have to be looked at now. Clearly those individuals whose profiles were already on the NDNAD could be excluded as they had not matched the suspect's part DNA profile.

But the rest would have to be traced so that voluntary DNA samples could be requested and profiles developed to compare with the killer's.

If all else failed and the killer was not identified, a new process then known as Familial DNA Searching (described in more detail later) would have to be considered.

The next development came when Norah's car was traced to a barn on a Canewdon farm. It was likely that the killer had touched the car and its contents since some of Norah's clothing had been found in the boot. Depending on its history post 1978, there was a outside possibility that more forensic work could be carried out. Unfortunately, enquiries revealed that it had passed through several hands since 1978. It was also in very poor condition, therefore unsuitable for any further forensic examination.

Then came the day we had all been waiting for. The monthly speculative search of the National DNA Database carried out in August 2004, produced a match with a forty nine year-old man. I still remember taking the telephone call from Forensic Scientist Judith Cunnison. I sat in silence, about to be given the name of the man who had killed Norah Trott. Would it be someone already identified as a possible suspect; or would it be a complete unknown? In some ways the situation was reminiscent of those TV shows where the winner is about to be revealed. Then there is a lengthy, unnecessary and rather annoying silence as the audience awaits the result with baited breath.

Judith did not put me through that, but it still seemed an eternity before she gave me the name, Wayne Philip Doherty. It was not a name I immediately recognised. The DNA profile had been developed from a sample he provided to Cambridge Police on the 4th July 2004, ironically my wedding anniversary! Doherty had been arrested for drink-driving in Cambridge and was now on bail pending his court appearance.

I was curious to know what his connection to Essex was if any; and whether or not his name had come up during the original investigation. When Judith had telephoned me, I was back working at Essex Police HQ in Chelmsford. I immediately drove to Rayleigh Police Station to re-examine the case papers.

I quickly discovered that in 1978, Wayne Doherty was living with his wife and their two children in Althorne Way, Canewdon. This is a village on the outskirts of Rochford. Interestingly, he used to frequent some of the public houses in Rochford town centre.

Records showed that within days of the murder, Doherty had gone to Germany where he was then working as a builder. He returned home for Christmas and was interviewed on the 18th December 1978, and again, on the 9th January 1979, mainly as part of the routine house-to-house enquiries. Like hundreds of other local men interviewed during those enquiries, Doherty was asked about his movements the evening that Norah was murdered. He told police he was not even in Rochford at the time of the killing and that he had actually been at home, decorating.

His then wife confirmed his alibi; but it is not clear how sure she was about his movements as some six weeks had elapsed since the murder. But then, how many wives could say with any degree of certainty exactly what their husbands had been doing six weeks before they were questioned about it?

Officers who saw Doherty also noted that he did not look like the artist's impression of the suspect; and his name did not appear on the comprehensive list of men who had been seen in and around the Rochford public houses on the night in question. They were therefore satisfied that he was not the killer.

Further research of Doherty's background revealed that in January 1980 (the year after his second police visit) Doherty committed another serious sexual offence only yards from Old Ship Lane. A woman had parked her car outside the Rochford Congregational Church in North Street and gone inside the church to collect her daughter from a Bible class. Thinking she would be quickly in and out, she left her two year old daughter in the car.

Doherty took the young child from the car and carried her to an isolated area nearby. There he indecently assaulted her.

On returning to her car, the woman found one of the doors open and her daughter missing. She screamed out in panic and on realising that the alarm had been raised, Doherty quickly abandoned the child. The area was searched and the girl was later found in darkness, on nearby wasteland. She was safely re-united with her mother.

Police enquiries revealed that Doherty had been seen in the area at the material time and he was arrested two days later. Doherty was subsequently charged with indecent assault and child stealing. Blood and saliva samples were routinely taken from him and his blood group was later found to match that of Norah's killer. But then, the same blood group probably matched thousands of other young men in and around Essex. Furthermore, the offence for which he had been arrested had been committed against a very young child rather than a woman in her 60's. Consequently, it appears that he was not seriously considered as a possible suspect for Norah Trott's murder.

Doherty was subsequently tried at Southend Crown Court where, on the 9th July 1980, he was sentenced to fifteen months imprisonment for indecent assault. The charge of child stealing was to 'lie on file'. When jailing him, Judge John Taylor said, 'To indecently assault this little child and then to abandon her in the hours of darkness in a place from which she could not escape was a loathsome thing.'

Having now identified Doherty as the prime suspect for Norah Trott's rape and murder, the re-investigation was allocated to the Rayleigh Major Investigations Team and became 'Operation Eccentric'. The Senior Investigating Officer (SIO) was Temporary Detective Superintendent Peter 'Nobby' Clark. As a young detective constable, Nobby had also worked on the original investigation. Coincidentally, Nobby was now approaching his retirement from the police service and had already secured a job as the third member of the Review Team.

Having the possible offender's name was a big step forward, but months of work still lay ahead. Nobby's successor, Detective Superintendent Simon Dinsdale, was later to say, 'The real issue for this case has been translating a 1970's investigation into a 21st century investigation under all the new rules of evidence, court procedure and disclosure.'

He described how it had taken a team of detectives three months to assess over 10,000 pieces of information and to trace and re-interview dozens of the original witnesses, one of whom had since moved to Australia! Important statements and other documents had also to be recorded onto the major investigations computer system, HOLMES. All physical evidence had once again to be reviewed to see it provided any further forensic opportunities.

Perhaps worryingly, photographs of Doherty taken around the time of Norah's murder did not really match the artist's impression of the 'baby faced' murder suspect, confirming what the detectives who originally interviewed him had also thought. However, as previously observed, the 'baby faced' suspect may have been at the crime scene, but he was not necessarily the killer.

By October 2004, detectives had enough evidence to arrest and charge Doherty with the rape and murder of Norah Trott. A warrant for his arrest was issued by Southend Magistrates Court and on the 8th October 2004, Doherty was arrested on Guernsey where he was then working as a builder. He was flown back to England and interviewed about the killing, but made no admissions. Two days later he was charged with Norah Trott's murder and remanded in custody.

Doherty's two week trial began at Basildon Crown Court in November 2005. By then the SIO, Nobby Clark, had actually retired and management of the case had transferred to Detective Superintendent Dinsdale. Ever loyal, Norah's ex-husband Ronald, now eighty four years-old, travelled up from his Devon home and was in court throughout the trial. Also present throughout the trial was a close personal friend of Norah's sister Teresa. She had felt it important that Teresa was represented. The woman, who wished to remain anonymous, later told the press that Teresa, who had died some ten years before, had been really close to Norah and never really got over her death.

The lead prosecutor was Martyn Levett (now a circuit judge); Doherty was represented by Michael Wolkind QC. Both were very experienced and successful barristers.

The trial mainly centered on the DNA evidence. The prosecution case was that DNA recovered from intimate samples obtained during the post mortem examination, together with other DNA recovered from semen found on Norah Trott's skirt, matched Wayne Doherty. Mr. Levett said there was a 1 in 190 million chance of the DNA found on Mrs Trott's clothing not belonging to Doherty and a one in 180,000 chance of the DNA found on her body belonging to someone other than Doherty.

The science behind DNA was carefully explained to the jury by the prosecutor, the forensic scientists who gave evidence and the trial judge his Honour Judge Philip Clegg. It was important that the jury understood the significance of the DNA evidence.

It reminded me of an occasion when, as a young detective, I investigated my first case of fraud. My old detective sergeant emphasized just how important it was to make sure the jury always understood what they were being told, however complicated. Otherwise, he said, juries will approach their final deliberations on the basis of, 'If in doubt, chuck it out!' I am sure that this is as true today, especially now that juries are often required to consider detailed technical and forensic evidence.

In this case, the prosecution also had to satisfy the jury that the biological material recovered during the post mortem examination and from Norah's clothing, could not have been accidentally contaminated by any biological material emanating from Doherty. In particular, the Forensic Science Service had to show that, once obtained, the samples associated with Norah Trott had been securely preserved and their movements from laboratory to laboratory, scientist to scientist, could be tracked over the past twenty five years. Fortunately that work had already been carried out during the review.

The jury listened attentively and after considering all the evidence decided that Doherty was indeed guilty of the rape and murder of Norah Trott.

On the 16th November 2005, his Honour Judge Clegg sentenced Doherty (now aged 50 years) to life imprisonment for Norah's murder. He said that Doherty was to serve at least twenty three years (less the time spent on remand awaiting trial) before even being considered for release.

Doherty was given a concurrent sentence of ten year imprisonment for raping Norah and would also be on the Sex Offenders Register for life.

Doherty stood silently as Judge Clegg very strongly and very publicly castigated him. His Honour paid tribute to Norah who, he said, was a charming woman who enjoyed life and made other people happy; yet she had been murdered in the most humiliating circumstances.

The Judge, referring to the murder and the subsequent attack on the two year-old child, told Doherty that he was at that time, a very dangerous man from whom the public needed to be protected. Judge Clegg was satisfied that Doherty formed his plan of attack shortly after 6pm. His conclusions were based on witness evidence concerning the young man seen hanging around opposite Norah's shop on the evening of the murder. Doherty, he continued, then lay in wait to attack her and had stamped on her voice box to prevent her screaming. Finally, Doherty had dragged Norah into an alleyway before violently raping and murdering her. Doherty's motivation, he said, was 'lust fuelled by drink.'

Judge Clegg then commended the police officers and forensic scientists involved in this investigation over the years, for their dedication and perseverance in finally bringing Doherty to justice. He also hoped that it would bring a degree of resolution to those who had been grieving for so many years.

Outside the court, Detective Superintendent Dinsdale told reporters it was sad that there were no surviving relatives and few surviving friends of Norah to witness the successful conclusion of the investigation. But he was sure the result would give hope to many others who are waiting for similar answers; and would put fear in the minds of those responsible for other unsolved crimes.

Ronald Trott described it as, 'A great day for forensic science and justice.' He went on to say, 'No one can bring Norah back to enjoy the happy retirement she was looking forward to, but convicting her vicious killer is the next best thing. Her death left a gap in our family life.'

Sadly, Doherty's seventy two year-old mother was unable to accept what her son had done. She told reporters that he was innocent and had been blamed for something he had not done. Her views about his 1980 conviction for indecently assaulting the two year-old child are unknown; but there is something touching about a mother's love for her child no matter what he did or did not do.

The final word went to Nobby Clark who was overjoyed with the verdict. He is reported to have told the press that it was not only justice for Norah, but for the people of Rochford who now knew who the killer was. 'She suffered terrible injuries and that made me feel vengeful. I was a Southend boy – it was my area, so it was personal.'

CHAPTER 4
ESSEX POLICE MAJOR CRIME REVIEW TEAM

In August 2003, Essex Police established its dedicated Major Crime Review Team at Police Headquarters, Chelmsford. The two founder members were the author and Peter Hamilton, both retired Detective Chief Inspectors (DCI's). During the next few years the team was joined by ex-DCI Peter 'Nobby' Clark; former Detective Inspector (DI) Gary Glassfield, former Detective Sergeants (DS) Brian 'Knocker' White and Phil Parker; finally, by the Review Team Manager, ex-Detective Superintendent (DSU) Kevin Macey.

We had all begun our police careers as uniformed constables, before transferring to the Criminal Investigations Department (CID). During our service we were promoted through the ranks, occasionally (if briefly) returning to uniform duties along the way.

Throughout our service we all completed a variety of detective training courses and acquired experience in many areas of criminal investigation, including secondments to the Regional Crime Squad, Major Investigations, the Drugs and Serious Crime Squad, Criminal Intelligence, Special Branch, Child Abuse Investigations and Professional Standards, the latter department investigating allegations of police officers' and police staff misconduct. In total, the Review Team had over two hundred year's experience in policing and criminal investigations.

The team was mainly set up to review on-going unsolved major crimes such as murder and 'Stranger Rape'. Nevertheless, we soon assumed responsibility for 'Cold Case' reviews. An example of a 'Cold Case' review has already been provided in the previous chapters so I will now focus on reviews of 'live' unsolved major investigations.

In addition, the team now has a responsibility for conducting what are known as Part 8 Reviews, which are mainly reviews into the sudden deaths of children; also for Domestic Homicide Reviews. But it also takes on any other case that Chief Police Officers require reviewing.

In the past these have included Missing Persons Found Dead, Suicides and Fatal Industrial Accidents.

Insofar as Major Crime Reviews are concerned, each police force has its own review policies and procedures. Interestingly, most forces do not formally begin their reviews of unsolved 'live' investigation until twenty eight days have elapsed from the commission of the crime, albeit that their senior managers will look at each unfolding investigations as part of their day-to-day managerial function.

Essex Police, on the other hand, has always taken the view that an early formal review is preferable. Things can go wrong during the initial stages of any investigation and if those errors are not quickly identified and rectified, the investigation itself may be fatally flawed. Consequently, if a major crime has not been solved within three days, it will normally be the subject of an Initial (72 hours) Review. This is sometimes described as a 'quick and dirty' review because it must be urgently carried out, yet be thorough enough to identify any important lines of enquiry that are not being rigorously pursued, or other important action that may have been overlooked.

In essence, the Review Team seeks to confirm that the investigation is being properly managed, that all opportunities to resolve it (especially forensic opportunities) have been recognized and are being prioritised and pursued, that the investigation itself and the Incident Office supporting it, are being run in accordance with national guidelines; finally, that the Senior Investigating Officer (SIO) has sufficient trained staff and other resources to complete all reasonable tasks within an acceptable timeframe.

One example of the importance of an early Initial Review actually related to a Missing Persons Investigation. Seventeen year-old Natasha Coombs, an only child, was a popular girl who lived with her parents Joanne and Gary, in Dovercourt, Essex. Natasha had been going out with an eighteen year-old Manningtree lad, Joshua Brennan, but they had separated about two weeks before her disappearance.

On Friday 27th July 2007, Natasha travelled to Ipswich for a Chinese meal with her friends. Later that evening, Natasha tried to contact Joshua, but on telephoning his home she was only able to speak with his brother. He told Natasha that Joshua had gone to the cinema with a girl from the restaurant where he worked as a part-time waiter. Natasha was upset and later tried once again to speak to Joshua, but without success.

At 10.15pm, Natasha telephoned her parents telling them that she was on her way back by train and would get a taxi home from Dovercourt Station. However, as Natasha left her friends, she told them that she was going to her ex-boyfriend's home.

At 10.42pm, Natasha boarded a London bound train at Ipswich Railway Station. This was later confirmed by closed circuit television (CCTV). The first stop would be Manningtree Station.

At 11.19pm, an emotional Natasha made a further telephone call to her ex-boyfriend's home, this time speaking to his mother. Natasha said she was walking on a railway line between Ipswich and Manningtree and that if her ex-boyfriend did not call her, she would throw herself under the next train. Mrs Brennan calmed Natasha down, then immediately telephoned Natasha's parents to tell them about their daughter's call. Mr. Coombs drove to Manningtree Station and on not finding Natasha there, searched the surrounding area; but he could find no trace of his daughter.

The following morning (28.7.2007) Mrs Coombs reported Natasha missing. Essex Police began a missing person's investigation and subsequent enquiries revealed that Natasha's mobile phone had disappeared from the mobile phone network in the Manningtree area.

All MISPERS are assessed depending on the circumstances of their disappearance and any possible risk to life. The assessment determines how police will respond. Natasha was assessed as being a Medium Risk MISPER.

Police began their enquiries and searches, but strict rules govern the searching of railway lines because they can cause severe disruption to passengers and freight. In any event, railway tracks are dangerous places and for health and safety reasons only British Transport Police (BTP) officers were then permitted to carry out such searches.

Essex Police told the BTP that Natasha was missing and asked them to arrange for train drivers to visually check the local railway lines as they drove along. It was during this telephone call that a member of BTP's control room staff falsely stated that all trains were fitted with sensors which would alert a train driver should the train strike an object. This information was accepted at 'face value' and influenced Essex Police's decision making when they were identifying the search areas. In short, no train strikes had been reported, so it was thought that Natasha had not been hit by a train.

Instead, Essex Police focussed on other search areas and routine lines of enquiry; there was after all, no evidence that Natasha had actually alighted from the train (apart from what she had said during her last telephone call) so she could be anywhere. Police searched open spaces, areas of water and the force helicopter also checked the railway lines, but nothing was found.

The following day (29.7.2007) Essex Police asked the BTP to organise a search of the railway line and requested their Police Search Adviser (PoLSA) liaise with his or her Essex Police counterpart. Unfortunately, BTP did not accede to those requests, deciding instead that a visual search of the railway line by train drivers was sufficient. This was not challenged until after the investigation was passed to the Stanway Major Investigations Team.

An Initial Review was also ordered and Peter Hamilton carried this out. He quickly realised that searchers had still not 'cleared the ground beneath their feet'. The information provided by Mrs Brennan indicated that Natasha was walking along the railway track between Ipswich and Manningtree Stations, but the track itself had still not been properly searched by the police. He recommended that this be done as a priority.

The search by BTP officers commenced on the 2nd August 2007; however, it was a slow and meticulous process. This was partly because the line could only be closed for a limited time each day. Also, the officers were not just looking for a body; they were looking for anything that might have belonged to Natasha, like her mobile phone.

Their search ended on the 10th August 2007, when a train driver approaching Manningtree station from the Colchester direction reported seeing a piece of material believed to have been part of Natasha's skirt, lying beside the railway track. Natasha's dead body was subsequently found by officers. It was down a railway embankment some eighteen hundred metres from Manningtree Railway Station, under a canopy of trees and therefore not visible from the air. A post mortem examination determined that Natasha's injuries were consistent with her having been struck by a train.

Sadly, Natasha's death had a profound effect on her mother, Joanne, and on the 18th September 2007, she took her own life by lying across the railway line close to where Natasha had been found. Joanne had a strong belief in life after death and her husband believes that she killed herself in order to be with Natasha.

An Inquest into their deaths was held at Chelmsford Coroner's Court on the 12th November 2007. The jury heard evidence from Essex Police Detective Sergeant Rennie Chivers that he did not think Natasha was walking between the rails when she was struck by the train. He believed she had been walking alongside the track and was struck by a passing train. The jury returned a verdict of 'Accidental Death' in respect of Natasha and 'Suicide' in respect of her mother.

Natasha's father made a number of complaints against Essex Police and the British Transport Police. The complaints were referred to the Independent Police Complaints Commission (IPCC) who conducted their own investigation. The main findings were published in March 2009 and posted on the IPCC's web site.

The IPCC concluded that both police forces had failed to conduct thorough and timely searches for Natasha and that there had been a failure to properly check and to act upon the information held by Essex Police. They also found that search opportunities had been lost because Essex Police had failed to assert itself (in their dealings with the BTP).

The IPCC said that Natasha should have been treated as a High Risk Missing Person at the outset and if she had been, certain actions would have been taken much sooner. For example, CCTV footage would have been obtained, both from railway stations and trains; and trained search advisors and their teams would have been deployed to carry out physical searches of the tracks. In particular, the police should have obtained CCTV footage from a level crossing and from external, forward facing cameras on trains. It was only after her death that police found footage from the front of a train that showed Natasha walking along the railway line between Manningtree and Colchester Railway Stations.

The IPCC also commented on the unwieldy nature of Essex Police's Command and Control System (STORM) when used to manage MISPER incidents. As time passes and investigations progress, it becomes difficult for officers studying the incident record, to understand exactly what action has already been taken and what further work is still required.

Essex Police and a number of other forces now use a bespoke system for missing person's investigations known as COMPACT (COMmunity Policing And Case Tracking). This records full details of each MISPER and the circumstances of their disappearance. It also provides a 'toolkit' of suggested actions and lines of enquiry for investigating officers to consider, together with sections of the database record which can be used to document the results of enquiries, etc. And, when the missing person is found (as most MISPERS are) COMPACT records details of where they went during their period of absence and where they were eventually found. All this information is then available if they go missing again.

One of the IPCC's main conclusions was that the need to carry out an early search of the railway line had not been fully realised.

Finally, the IPCC found that information which was inappropriate, confidential and inaccurate had been passed to the media, including the Daily Mirror and the Sunday Mirror Unfortunately, they failed to identify the source of that information as the newspapers allegedly refused to reveal it.

Other complaints made by Mr. Coombs were unsubstantiated.

The IPCC could not determine if the delay in finding Natasha's body had been a factor in her mother's decision to commit suicide, although it had clearly caused her and the family additional stress and anxiety.

The IPCC published other key findings including the fact that what they referred to as a 'hasty search' of the railway line should have been carried out. By this they meant that an initial walk along the railway lines should have been undertaken, rather than the more thorough search that had taken some time to complete. A 'hasty search' may have located Natasha's body much earlier.

Essex Police accepted that there had been failings with this investigation, albeit that these had not affected the final outcome insofar as Natasha was concerned.

The IPPC recommended disciplinary proceedings be taken against the BTP control room operator who had provided false information to Essex Police. However, the operator resigned from the force so could not be disciplined. The IPCC also made a number of recommendations designed to improve the way police deal with such incidents in the future.

In my view, Natasha was probably already dead by the time she was reported missing; but her body could and should have been found earlier.

One could take the view that it should not have taken a 72 Hours Review, to realise the obvious. However, my own view is that those running the investigation had probably not wanted to 'put all their eggs in one basket' and kept all possible options open.

After all, once Natasha had finished her meal, she telephoned her parents saying she was on her way home; but shortly after she told her friends that she was going to her ex-boyfriend's home. It was always possible that something had happened to her en-route to either places, and possibly after leaving her last railway station. So in addition to trying to arrange a search of the railway track, officers also tried to cover other possibilities. They continued their routine enquiries and searches of other possible locations that she may have reached. The problem was that they were working so hard at the tasks they could achieve, that the difficulties they were experiencing with the BTP became secondary. The fact that the review procedure was in existence, ensured that the focus of the search activity was redirected back to the railway track.

The importance of an Initial Review was also demonstrated in the case of Daniel Batten, a twenty year-old Harlow man who was murdered in August 2003. Daniel was out with two friends when they were attacked by a group of Asian men. Two of the attackers had knives and Daniel died after receiving a single stab wound that penetrated his heart and lung. Detectives soon had a suspect, a local man named Imran Hussain; but they could not find him or the car he was believed to be using.

The murder pre-dated the now widespread use of ANPR (Automatic Number Plate Recognition) so the most that could be done to find the car was via regular briefings of police patrols. But that was a bit 'hit and miss'; it relied on police coming across the car during one of their patrols. The problem was that the longer this took, the less chance detectives had of recovering any forensic evidence from the suspect's car.

An Initial Review was conducted by Peter Hamilton who recommended, amongst other things, that police patrols were increased the following weekend so that every road, driveway and car park in the Harlow area could be systematically searched for Hussain's car.

As a result, the car was quickly found and Hussain arrested. Forensic scientist later found traces of Daniel's blood around the driver's seat, thus confirming Hussain's involvement.

In August 2004, Hussain was convicted of murder and sentenced to life imprisonment. He was ordered to serve a minimum of fifteen years in prison; this was later reduced on appeal, to a minimum of fourteen years.

Again, it could be argued that it should not have required a 72 Hours Review to solve the problem. But investigators were focussed on locating the suspect and his car via enquiries and visiting his known haunts; and they were probably quite optimistic about finding him as he was a local man. They had, therefore, not properly considered what they would do if they were unsuccessful.

Returning to the review process itself, generally speaking, each review will have a lead reviewer who will produce the final written report. But if necessary, the lead reviewer will be supported by other members of the team and / or specialist officers seconded to the review.

The reviewers will firstly be briefed by the Senior Investigating Officer (SIO) and key members of his or her team and may visit the crime scene itself. They will be shown relevant CCTV footage, photographs, maps, etc., and will be provided with copies of key witness statements and other important documents.

Reviewers will consider the forensic and all other aspects of the investigation, including the running of the Incident Office, the extent of house-to-house enquiries, CCTV opportunities, telephony, searches for evidence, media management and liaison with the victim's family. Any urgent action that should be considered will be verbally notified to the SIO and a formal report will be produced in due course.

Generally speaking, if the crime is still unsolved after twenty eight days, a more comprehensive review is then conducted. This necessitates reviewers reading all statements and other documents so far obtained or created on HOLMES. They will carry out an in-depth examination of all aspects of the investigation and will check to confirm that the SIO's instructions to his team are being followed.

Invariably recommendations will arise from the review. Some will relate to the investigation itself, others may relate to such issues as police training, equipment or procedures.

The operational recommendations will firstly be considered by the SIO. Usually, most are accepted, but the SIO is in charge of the investigation and may decide that a particular recommendation will not be pursued; or at least, will not be pursued at that stage of the investigation, but may be reconsidered later.

The recommendations will then be considered by a panel of senior officers at a Review Commission meeting. The Commission is given a briefing about the crime itself, the investigation and the findings of the review. They will then consider any investigative recommendations not adopted by the SIO. They can over-rule the SIO if they believe the decision not to pursue an investigative recommendation was wrong. The Commission is also in a position to progress any organisational or police service recommendations.

Periodic reviews will continue until the crime is solved or until the SIO considers that s/he has completed all reasonable lines of enquiry. The SIO then produces a Closing Report for consideration by the Review Team Manager and finally, by the Review Commission. The term 'Closing Report' is a misnomer as no unsolved major crime investigation is ever closed. In reality the investigation is inactive for a period of time pending any new information or evidence coming to light, or for two years, whichever is the sooner. When the case is next revisited the reviewers will consider, amongst other things, any new advances in forensic science or technology that might finally resolve the crime.

If the 'Cold Case' review identifies a suspect or other opportunities to finally resolve the crime, an updated review report will be prepared and the case once more submitted for re-investigation by a Major Investigations Team.

Until 2007, Essex Police had four Major Investigation Teams. However, in April 2007, the Police Authorities for Kent and Essex agreed to pursue a number of collaborative ventures.

These were designed to improve the quality of service, achieve better value for money and to ensure that their combined resources were used more effectively.

The Kent and Essex Serious Crime Directorate (SCD) was formed out of this collaborative venture, primarily to tackle serious and organised crime. In total the newly formed SCD had more than eleven hundred police officers and support staff working together across both counties. The SCD is responsible for the investigation of the most serious crimes, known as MARE offences i.e. Murder, Abduction, Rape and Extortion. They may also investigate attempts or conspiracies to murder, plus 'Stranger' and 'Serial Rapes'.

The Directorate currently has six permanent Major Investigations Teams (MIT's), three in Essex and three in Kent. Each team is led by an SIO and works from its own dedicated Incident Office. In addition, both forces have their own Major Crime Review Teams, both led by the Review Team Manager; plus operational 'Cold Case' Investigations Teams (CCIT), led by an SIO. The formation of the CCIT means that once a suspect for a previously unsolved major crime is identified by a Review Team, the CCIT can carry out the investigation, rather than it be allocated to a Major Investigation Team.

The CCIT will carry out further enquiries that will either eliminate the suspect from the investigation, or confirm our suspicions and pursue the investigation to a prosecution.

CHAPTER 5
THE ABDUCTION AND MURDER OF DINAH McNICOL

It was the summer of 1991, and eighteen year-old student Dinah McNicol was enjoying a break from her studies. She had just completed her 'A' levels and the results would help her decide whether she would go on to university, or spend the next couple of years travelling. Dinah lived with her father and brother in Tillingham, a small village not far from the now City of Chelmsford.

Had Dinah grown up during the 1960's, she might have been described as a 'hippy'. She made her own clothes and jewellery; and enjoyed the outdoor life, happy to 'rough it' at music festivals and similar events. In fact, officers later investigating her disappearance made enquiries at a number of 'hippy' communes and peace camps.

But unlike most students, Dinah was quite well off financially with over £2,000 in the bank, a not inconsiderable sum in 1991. But Dinah knew that the next few years would be financially challenging so she spent her money wisely. When visiting friends or relatives she would always work out the most economical way of travelling, arranging lifts where she could or even hitch-hiking.

Saturday 3rd August 1991 was no different. Dinah intended spending the weekend at a music festival at Liphook in Hampshire. Ordinarily she would have travelled there with her friends, but by chance she found that an acquaintance would be visiting his family in Hampshire that weekend so she arranged a lift to the festival with him. That afternoon, Dinah arrived at the festival site where she met up with her friends. She then spent the rest of the weekend with them.

On Sunday afternoon (4.8.1991) Dinah went for a walk around the festival site and met a young man. They struck up a conversation and seemed to get on well; and when she returned to her friends, he was also with her. Dinah's friends had planned on returning home later that day, but Dinah decided to stay for one more night with her new companion. Dinah mentioned that she might then hitchhike to nearby Portsmouth as she had never been there before.

But the following day (5.8.1991) Dinah decided to hitchhike home; and as her new-found companion was travelling in the same direction to their respective homes, they left the festival site together and headed for the A3.

Dinah never reached home, but her disappearance was not immediately realised. Her father had gone away for a few weeks at the end of July and it was not until his return that the family realised Dinah was missing. Police were eventually informed on the 30th August 1991. At first they dealt with this incident as a routine missing person's investigation. Dinah's home was searched as a matter of course and her 'A' level results were found, unopened.

Relatives and friends were interviewed and house-to-house enquiries carried out locally; all to no avail. Dinah had simply disappeared. Police also made enquiries of Dinah's bank. They found that between the 8th and 27th August 1991, numerous cash withdrawals had been made from her account via automatic cash-point machines at various locations along the south coast i.e. Hove, Brighton, Portslade, Margate and Ramsgate. Whilst this appeared out of character, Dinah's card had not been reported lost or stolen and her PIN was being used to access her account.

Within days, the investigation was being supervised by a local CID officer, Detective Sergeant Derek Nickol. He became increasingly concerned for Dinah's welfare and during the years that followed (right up to his retirement) he kept the investigation alive. During this time DS Nickol regularly briefed senior officers and pursued all reported sightings of Dinah and other lines of enquiry including media appeals, plus checks of various agencies and organisations. But he found nothing to show that Dinah was still alive.

Interestingly, one such media appeal resulted in a witness coming forward who told police that he had seen a young woman fitting Dinah's description in the village of Grayshott (near Liphook) the morning she had left the music festival. The woman was with a young man. Another potential witness also told police that in early August 1991, they had seen a woman fitting Dinah's description making a cash withdrawal from a bank machine in Ramsgate, Kent.

(Ramsgate was one of the towns that cash withdrawals from Dinah's account had been made.)

Two other witnesses reported having given a young woman a lift from Southminster to Chelmsford on the 24th August 1991. They did not know Dinah, but their description of her, and the content of their conversations with her during the journey, led them to believe that the passenger was indeed Dinah McNicol. If those witnesses were right, Dinah was alive, well and voluntarily absent from home. Just the same, it was still a matter of concern that there had been no sightings of Dinah by anyone who actually knew her, after the 4th August 1991.

The first real breakthrough came following a Crimewatch appeal on the 14th September 1992, just over a year after Dinah's disappearance. Dinah's travelling companion was identified as David Tremlett from Reigate in Surrey. He confirmed that both he and Dinah had left the festival together, buying some food at Grayshott, before hitching a lift along the A3 towards London. He said that the first motorist to pick them up had dropped them off at a location known as The Devil's Punchbowl.

They were then picked up by a white, middle-aged man, described as being in his late thirties to early forties, with straw coloured, wavy hair. He was driving alone in a small, old, four door car, possibly green in colour and which had a child's seat inside.

The only other things Mr Tremlett could remember about the driver were that he had blue-grey eyes and spoke with what he thought was a mild west country accent. However, he admitted that he could not hear the driver properly because it was a warm day, the car windows were open and the car was travelling quite fast.

Mr Tremlett said that Dinah had declined an invitation to go home with him. He said they had eventually parted company at the Reigate turn-off, Junction 8 of the M25. Dinah stayed in the front passenger seat of the car and, as far as he knew, Dinah's intention was to continue her journey home. Before they parted, Dinah gave Mr Tremlett her telephone number and though he did try to contact her several times, he was unsuccessful. This was the last confirmed sighting of Dinah, alive.

There was no reason to disbelieve Mr Tremlett; so had Dinah arrived home later that day and then disappeared from Essex? Or did the answer lie with the unknown driver who had given them a lift from The Devil's Punchbowl; or perhaps with someone else who later picked Dinah up during her journey home?

In 2007, Essex Police decided to review the investigations of a number of long-term missing persons. Dinah McNicol's case would be reviewed by Nobby Clark. He immediately recognised the difficulties that had been faced by the original investigators. Dinah was living in Essex, but she was last seen in Surrey en-route from a music festival in Hampshire. Cash withdrawals had been made from her account at various locations on the South Coast and after those withdrawals there had been at least one possible sighting of Dinah back in Essex. Where do you start looking?

Nobby studied the case papers and amongst them found references to a man named Peter Tobin. During the early 1990's, Tobin had frequented towns along the south coast of England. Then, in 1993, Tobin was imprisoned for abducting, raping and attempting to murder two schoolgirls.

Furthermore, enquiries revealed that following his release from prison in 2004, Tobin had returned to his birthplace, Scotland, where he had just been convicted of the rape and murder of a young Polish woman, Angelika Kluk. Her dead body had been found buried under the floor of a church.

But Tobin was said to have a broad Scottish accent so could not be the man described by David Tremlett; unless Mr Tremlett had been mistaken about the driver's west country accent. It would be necessary to fully enquire into Tobin's background.

Peter Britton Tobin was born on the 27th August 1946, in Renfrewshire, Scotland. As he grew up, Tobin drifted into petty crime and spent time in an approved school and a young offender's institute. In 1969, Tobin moved with his seventeen year-old girlfriend Margaret, to Brighton, Sussex, where they married.

But the relationship did not last long; the couple separated in 1970, and were divorced the following year.

In 1973, whilst still living in Brighton, Tobin met and married a nurse, Sylvia. They had two children, but one died at birth. That marriage was also short lived, only lasting until 1976 when Sylvia left her husband, taking their son with her.

Tobin's next relationship was with Cathy who gave birth to their son in December 1987. She was just seventeen year-old when, two years later, they married in Brighton.

In 1990, the Tobin family moved to Bathgate in West Lothian, Scotland; but they separated when Cathy returned to her original hometown of Portsmouth. Tobin wanted to be near his son so in May 1991, he moved to Margate in Kent and from there to Havant, Hampshire, some two years later.

In August 1993, two fourteen year old girls came to Tobin's flat, to babysit his young son. There, he allegedly held them at knifepoint and forced them to drink cider and vodka. He then committed serious sexual assaults on them, before turning on the gas taps and leaving them for dead. Tobin then went on the run. Living under a false name he joined a religious sect in Coventry, but was subsequently arrested after his car was seen in Brighton.

On the 18th May 1994, at Winchester Crown Court, he pleaded guilty to various charges and was sent to prison for fourteen years.

In 2004, Tobin was released from prison and moved back to Renfrewshire. He then moved to Glasgow assuming the name 'Pat McLaughlin'. At that time he was still a Registered Sex Offender and should have informed police of his new address; but he failed to do so and the following year a warrant was issued for his arrest.

By 2006, Peter Tobin, alias 'Pat McLaughlin' had secured a job as the handyman at the St Patrick's Roman Catholic Church in Anderson, Glasgow. Also working there was a twenty three year-old Polish student, Angelika Kluk. She was actually staying at the presbytery whilst working as a cleaner to finance her Scandinavian studies.

Tobin befriended her and she was last seen alive, in his company, on the 24th September 2006. Three days later her dead body was found under floorboards beneath the confessional in St Patrick's Church. Angelika had been beaten, stabbed and raped. Worse still, forensic evidence indicated that she may have still been alive when her body was left there.

Strathclyde Police launched a murder enquiry led by Detective Superintendent David Swindle. 'Pat McLaughlin' was routinely interviewed, but detectives really became suspicious when he suddenly left the area. They discovered his true identity and learnt of his previous convictions. He became their main suspect.

Once again, Tobin went on the run, but he was traced to London where he had been admitted to hospital with a fictitious illness, under yet another false name. He was arrested and subsequently charged with Angelika's murder.

In March 2007, his trial before Lord Menzies took place at the High Court of Justiciary in Edinburgh. The prosecution was led by Dorothy Bain QC Advocate Depute (the highest-ranking prosecutorial position in Scotland). Tobin was represented by Donald Findlay QC. The trial was to last six weeks. Tobin (now sixty years of age) denied raping and murdering Angelika, but claimed that she had had consensual sex with him. He was found guilty and sentenced to life imprisonment.

Lord Menzies described him as an 'evil man' and ordered that he serve a minimum of twenty one years before his release could even be considered. He would be over eighty years-old by then.

Detective Superintendent Swindle suspected that Tobin was responsible for other serious crimes and co-ordinated enquiries across the United Kingdom as part of 'Operation Anagram'. The day following Tobin's conviction, police announced plans to interview Tobin about the disappearance of fifteen year-old Vicky Hamilton, who in 1991, went missing from Bathgate, West Lothian, where Tobin was then living. Could he also be responsible for Vicky's disappearance?

Vicky Hamilton disappeared on the 10th February 1991. She was returning to her home in Redding, near Falkirk, by bus, having spent the weekend in Livingstone with her sister Sharon.

Sharon later recalled that Vicky had really enjoyed their weekend together and was looking forward to returning the following weekend. Around 5pm, the sisters said their goodbyes at the bus stop where Vicky's journey home began. It involved travelling to the town of Bathgate, where she was last seen eating chips whilst waiting for her next bus. That bus stop was only a mile or so from Peter Tobin's Bathgate home in Robertson Avenue.

When Vicky failed to arrive home, her mother immediately called the police and this led to one of the biggest missing persons investigations ever conducted in Scotland. During their investigation police took over three thousand witness statements and spoke to over six and a half thousand people.

On the 21st February 1991, Vicky's purse was found some twenty miles away in St Andrew's Square, Edinburgh. It had been dumped in a gutter under a portable building. The purse was dry and the contents were intact. The location was not far from the main railway and bus stations and detectives later surmised that it had been left there to mislead police into thinking that Vicky had simply run away.

On the 21st March 1991, Tobin moved from the Bathgate home he had lived in since 1990, to Margate in Kent.

Sadly, in January 1993, Vicky's mother Jeanette died without ever knowing what had happened to her daughter.

The search for Vicky continued on and off for many years and in February 2001, police re-launched their investigation. Ten years had passed since Vicky's disappearance.

Then, in November 2006, police launched a fresh investigation hoping that advances in DNA testing could be applied to the re-examination of Vicky's purse.

On the 4th June 2007, soon after Tobin's conviction for the murder of Angelika Kluk, police began a search of Tobin's former Bathgate home.

In the attic they found a dagger with a five inch long blade. DNA analysis of a small piece of skin found on the blade showed that it matched Vicky Hamilton's DNA profile.

The examination of Vicky's discarded purse also revealed a DNA profile that matched Tobin's young son. Had Tobin given it to his son to play with?

When Tobin was interviewed by detectives, he admitted that the knife was his. But he could not (or would not) give an explanation as to how a piece of Vicky's skin ended up on his knife; nor how the knife had ended up in his loft. Tobin was also unable (or unwilling) to explain how his son's DNA had been found on Vicky's purse.

On the 21st July 2007, Tobin was charged with the murder of Vicky Hamilton although police had still not found her body.

As Tobin awaited trial for Vicky Hamilton's murder, the review of Dinah McNicol case continued. By now, Nobby Clarke was liaising with an Essex Police Senior Investigating Officer (SIO), Detective Superintendent Tim Wills of Stanway Major Investigations Team. Both were in regular contact with their Scots colleagues. They studied maps of the south coast and realised this was an area that Tobin had probably been quite familiar with in 1991.

Tobin was then living at 50 Irvine Drive, Margate, but regularly visiting his young son, who was living with his mother in Portsmouth, Hampshire. Tobin would know the main routes to and from those locations, which could include sections of the A3, plus the various coastal routes along which were several of the cash machines that had been used to withdraw money from Dinah's account.

Nobby also became aware of some information provided by Tobin's former next door neighbour from number 52 Irvine Drive, David Martin. He said that Tobin was a normal man and talking to him was '...like talking to your best mate or someone down the pub.' Importantly, Mr Martin recalled an unusual incident that began to trouble the officers.

He said that one day he was looking over the fence and saw Tobin digging a massive hole in his back garden. He joked with Tobin saying, 'Are you going for Australia?' Tobin replied saying he was digging a sand-pit for when his son stayed with him. Despite this explanation, within days the hole had been filled in and the ground leveled off.

Had Dinah's body been buried in Tobin's garden? There was only one way to find out.

In November 2007, arrangements were made for the occupants of 50 Irvine Drive to be temporarily re-housed whilst police search teams and forensic scientists began a search of the property utilising specialist search equipment. After a preliminary survey of the house and garden, the site of the 'sand-pit' was excavated. There, police discovered that a thin layer of cement had been poured over and around the edge of the 'sand pit'. The soil below it was then removed revealing some black plastic bin liners. The bags contained a partially clothed, dismembered body, later confirmed to be that of Vicky Hamilton. It was wrapped in several layers of plastic bags and cloth. Vicky was still wearing her mother's rings. Fingerprints recovered from one of the bin liners matched those of Peter Tobin.

A post mortem examination of Vicky's body failed to establish exactly how she had died, but intimate swabs of her body appeared to contain Tobin's DNA, suggesting that Vicky may have been subjected to a sexual assault by Tobin. Toxicology revealed traces of Amitriptyline, an anti-depressant which can act as a sedative. Tobin had been prescribed similar medication prior to Vicky's disappearance.

This, together with the evidence recovered from Tobin's knife and Vicky's purse, led detectives to conclude that Vicky had probably been abducted, drugged and sexually assaulted by Tobin. He had then killed and dismembered her at his Bathgate home, using the knife later found in his loft. They further suspected that he later drove her body to Margate for burial in his back garden.

I recall that when first informed of the discovery, I was a little disappointed that it was not Dinah McNicol's body; we were all sure she was dead.

But I quickly realised that the mystery of another young girl's disappearance had now been finally solved and that Vicky's body would soon be returned to her family in Scotland. Vicky's funeral was held at her former local church in Redding on the 30th November 2007.

The search of the garden continued and Dinah's body was subsequently found buried in another part of it. Traces of anti-depressant drugs and other medication for sleeping disorders were also found in her body. Again, similar medication had also previously been prescribed to Tobin. Clearly Dinah had suffered a similar fate to Vicky Hamilton; and at the hands of the same killer.

A decision was taken that the two murders would be tried separately (England and Scotland have different legal systems). In September 2008, the Crown Prosecution Service served a summons on solicitors acting for Peter Tobin, accusing him of Dinah's murder.

Tobin's trial for the murder of Vicky Hamilton began on the 3rd November 2008, before Lord Emslie, at the High Court in Dundee. Tobin was again defended by Donald Findlay QC. The prosecution was led by Frank Mulholland QC, then the Solicitor General for Scotland. (He subsequently became the Lord Advocate and a Member of the Privy Council.)

The evidence against Tobin was overwhelming. Most damming of all were the facts that Vicky's body had been recovered from the back garden of his former Margate home; his fingerprints were on the plastic bag containing parts of her body; his DNA was recovered from swabs of her body and a piece of her skin had been found on his knife, recovered from his former Bathgate home. Finally, Tobin's young son's DNA profile was also found on Vicky's discarded purse.

Despite all this evidence, he pleaded 'Not Guilty' and a four week trial followed.

On the 2nd December 2008, the jury, having retired to consider their verdict, took three hours to convict Tobin of Vicky's murder.

When sentencing him Lord Emslie said, 'You stand convicted of the truly evil abduction and murder of a vulnerable young girl in 1991 and thereafter of attempting to defeat the ends of justice in various ways over an extended period. Yet again you have shown yourself to be unfit to live in a decent society. It is hard for me to convey the loathing and revulsion that ordinary people will feel for what you have done. I fix the minimum period which you must spend in custody at 30 years. Had it been open to me I would have made that period run consecutive to the 21 year custodial period that you are already serving.'

Tobin was by then sixty two years of age, so will now be in his nineties before he could even be considered for release.

Tobin did not just attract the loathing and revulsion of ordinary people for whilst in prison a fellow inmate (a convicted rapist) slashed Tobin's face and neck with a razor. He said that Tobin had been annoying him for months because of his (Tobin's) attitude towards his offences and refusal to tell anyone where the rest of the victims' bodies are.

Even convicted rapists have standards!

During the month following Tobin's conviction, he gave notice of appeal. It appears that Tobin considered his sentence to be excessive; however, he did not pursue the appeal.

In June 2009, Tobin's trial for the murder of Dinah McNicol began, but he suddenly became ill and was hospitalised. The trial was abandoned pending his recovery.

On the 14th December 2009, at Chelmsford Crown Court, before Mr Justice Calvert-Smith, Tobin finally stood trial for the murder of Dinah McNicol. Once again, despite the overwhelming evidence (and the fact that he had by now been convicted of two similar murders) Tobin pleaded not guilty. Nevertheless, he offered no evidence in his defence and after a three day trial the jury, having retired for only fifteen minutes, unanimously found him guilty.

Again, he was sentenced to life imprisonment, but this time the judge told him that in this case, life would mean life.

Sentencing him the judge said, 'This is the third time you have stood in the dock for murder. On all three occasions the evidence against you was overwhelming. Yet even now you refuse to come to terms with your guilt.'

He also commented that Tobin's refusal to co-operate with the police had meant that the family knew nothing about the circumstances of Dinah's death.

Speaking after the trial, Dinah's half-sister Sarah said that at least after all these years the family knew the truth about Dinah's disappearance and believed that justice had prevailed. She said that the family would remember Dinah as the unique and inspiring person that she was.

Detective Superintendent Wills said, 'Rarely matters come before courts in this country that demonstrate human behavior that is so self-serving and evil. I will finish my day at work satisfied that he will never walk free again amongst the communities he committed such vile acts against. Peter Tobin I can only describe as pure evil. He has shown no remorse for killing Dinah or any of the other women he has been convicted of killing.'

The final word went to the officer who expended so much time and energy in trying to resolve Dinah's disappearance, ex-Detective Sergeant Derek Nickol. He said, 'Satisfaction is a difficult word in these circumstances, but I am delighted now that this has been resolved. Many years ago the evidence was not there. But I always held out hope.'

Detective Superintendent David Swindle, of Strathclyde Police, who set up Operation Anagram to investigate Tobin's background, said the investigation would continue even after Tobin's death.

He said: 'Peter Tobin has now been found guilty for the brutal murders of three young women. Who knows if he has killed others? No stone will be left unturned and every single piece of information gathered will be investigated by forces throughout the UK to establish if he was responsible for any other crimes.'

After his last trial, police continued to investigate Tobin's possible involvement in other serious crimes, including murder, some of which he has allegedly boasted about in prison. They have also released photographs of over thirty unidentified items of jewellery which they fear were taken by Tobin from other victims, possibly as trophies.

In 2011, Operation Anagram began to 'wind down'. However, Detective Superintendent Swindle said anyone with information regarding Peter Tobin would still be able to contact the Anagram incident room via e-mail which would be monitored daily.

CHAPTER 6
THE MURDER OF JEAN DICKER

The murders recounted so far were very difficult to resolve, mainly because unlike most homicides, the killers and their victims were unknown to each other; and the killings themselves were completely random.

Sometimes it is difficult to know where to start with any criminal investigation, so I was surprised to have Rudyard Kipling quoted to me when I attended my first detective training course! The following is an extract from his poem 'The Elephant's Child'.

'I keep six honest serving-men,

(they taught me all I knew).

Their names are

What and Why and When and How and Where and Who?'

In other words:

What has happened?

Why did it happen?

When did it happen?

How did it happen?

Where did it happen?

Answer those questions and you should be able to answer the final question - 'Who?'

Fortunately (for investigators) most homicides are committed by offenders who know their victims and / or who are known by their victims. They may, for example, be relatives, friends or work colleagues; or there may be some other link. They, perhaps, travelled the same route to work, maybe on the same bus or train; or frequented the same pubs or clubs. Or they may have mutual friends, interests or hobbies which somehow link them.

For this reason, one of the most important lines of enquiry in any major investigation, but especially murder, is the 'victimology'. Detectives will try to find out everything they can about the victim, including their most recent and last movements; but especially about their public and private lives. They will seek this from the victim's family, friends and associates who will be questioned about the victim's state of health, daily routines, the vehicles they drive or have access to, details of their finances, education, employment, hobbies and interests. The list is not exhaustive.

Detectives will also be interested in the different methods of communication the victim used, for example, telephones, e-mail, computers, Skype, social networking, etc., and any significant events in their lives. At the same time the police will check their own and other agencies' records to see what else, if anything, is known about the victim.

In most cases a link, albeit tenuous, will be found between the offender and the victim. Consequently, once the full victimology has been obtained the Senior Investigating Officer (SIO) can be reasonably certain that the name of the offender probably lies within all the information gathered. This obviously gives the SIO 'a starter for ten'.

But even having a short list of those who *could* be responsible does not necessarily make the task of identifying the offender and proving their guilt any easier. This was the dilemma that faced detectives investigating the murder of Jean Dicker.

In January 2003, Jean, a fifty eight year-old retired traffic warden, was living with her thirty four year-old son Steven, in a bungalow in Craigfield Avenue, Clacton-on-Sea. She had been happily married to her husband Len for many years, but sadly he had died of cancer the previous May. Len's death had a profound effect on Jean who felt she could no longer live without him. In July 2002, having decided to take her own life, Jean wrote a number of letters setting out her wishes, including the fact that Steven should inherit the bungalow.

Jean also had a daughter, Tracy; she was married and living in her own home some twenty miles away at Stanway, on the outskirts of Colchester.

Jean also had two brothers, both of whom were married. She was in regular contact with them and their respective wives.

There is no doubt that Jean had intended to commit suicide that July; her's was not simply 'a cry for help'. And it was fortunate indeed that she was found alive.

During the next few weeks, Jean was an in-patient at a local mental health unit, eventually recovering sufficiently to enable her discharge back into the community under supervision. But the family still had concerns for her, so Steven moved back to live with his mother. That way she would not be so lonely and he could keep a closer eye on her.

As part of her rehabilitation, Jean was encouraged to pursue various interest including bowling, relaxation and art classes. She also owned two dogs, Dachshunds 'Flame' and 'Fern'. They were both friendly and well behaved so Jean had high hopes of their soon being accepted as 'PAT' (Pets as Therapy) dogs. She could then take them into hospitals and care homes to help improve patients' and residents' health and quality of life.

Steven also owned a dog, a Cocker Spaniel named 'Sunny'. Steven had previously been married and had three children. Unfortunately, things did not work out and the couple had separated.

In due course, Steven met another woman and had planned on moving back with her once he was sure that Jean could cope with living on her own.

Steven worked for a local engineering company in Stephenson Road, Great Clacton. He had previously been unemployed for a long period of time, so the job was very important to him. His normal routine, Monday to Friday, was to get up around 7am, get ready for work and drive there in his Ford Escort for an 8am start. He usually worked through the day until 6pm, arriving back home about ten minutes later.

Steven would usually have dinner with Jean, then spend the rest of the evening at home. He mainly saw his girlfriend at weekends.

Tracy also stayed in close contact with her mother and would frequently speak to Steven about Jean's health and general well-being.

According to Steven, Wednesday 29th January 2003, started out no differently to any other working day; sadly, it ended with his mother being beaten to death in their home.

Steven later told police that on that day he had arrived home from work as usual, around 6.10pm. Soon after arriving home and as he was talking to his mother, his Aunty May telephoned Jean. The two women then chatted for a while. Afterwards, Steven resumed his conversation with Jean. He recalled that the conversation with his mother (including her telephone conversation with Aunty May) had lasted around forty five minutes.

Steven said he then went to the toilet, had a wash and brush up, made Jean a cup of tea and then left home around 7.45pm to visit his friend, Gary. He told police that he had stopped twice whilst en-route to Gary's; firstly to visit Gary's mother, then at an off-licence near Gary's home where he bought some alcohol.

Steven then went on to say that once at Gary's home, the pair had spent the evening drinking and smoking whilst watching a film on TV. Once the film had ended, Steven went home as he had to be up for work the next day.

Again, according to Steven, he arrived back home around 11.20pm. He unlocked the front door and on entering discovered Jean's dead body at the far end of the 'L' shaped hallway. He could see that she had been badly beaten around the head and that blood was splattered on the surrounding walls and doors. The three dogs were barking in the kitchen, but as Jean's body was blocking the kitchen door, he could only reach them by going through the computer room. This would then allow him access to the kitchen.

Steven dialled '999' and shortly after police officers and paramedics arrived at the bungalow. He later told the police that whilst making the '999' call he had vomited. The ambulance crew examined Jean's body. They could find no pulse, albeit that her body was still warm to the touch.

The police officers looked around, checking the exhaust pipe on Steven's car in the process. They found it was cold and began to wonder whether or not he had been telling the truth when he said he had only just arrived home. The officers checked the bungalow and found no sign of a forced entry. They also established that Steven was the last person to have seen his mother alive that evening; and was the one who had found her dead.

They began to have further doubts about what Steven had told them and arrested him on suspicion of murder. However, when the local Detective Inspector arrived on scene, he was not satisfied that there was enough suspicion to justify Steven's continued detention, so ordered his immediate release. Instead, Steven was to be treated as a significant witness.

He was taken to Clacton Police Station and his clothing removed for forensic examination. Such action is routine where an individual has entered a crime scene, especially if they may have come into contact with the victim. This is because there is a risk that items left by the offender, such as fibres, hairs, DNA, etc., can be accidentally picked up on the witness' clothing or shoes and lost from the crime scene; also, that such items can be innocently left at the crime scene by the witness, causing unnecessary confusion. For this reason any shoes or clothing worn by the witness at a major crime scene may be seized and preserved for forensic examination.

A major crime investigation was launched by the Senior Investigating Officer (SIO) Detective Superintendent (later Chief Constable) Gareth Wilson of Stanway Major Investigations Team (MIT). Steven was taken to a local hotel since he would not be allowed back into his home until it had been forensically examined and thoroughly searched. This was likely to take several days. During this time he was questioned by police in order to help compile the victimology.

At the same time Steven, like other close relatives and friends of Jean's, was asked to fully account for his movements during the period leading up to and following the murder. Where possible, their individual accounts and alibis would be independently verified.

Forensic scientists attended the crime scene and a post mortem examination was later carried out by a Home Office Forensic Pathologist. The cause of death was found to be multiple head injuries, which were probably inflicted in the hallway where Jean's body was subsequently found.

The bungalow and surrounding area were later searched, but the murder weapon was not recovered.

Detectives considered a number of possible scenarios, known as hypotheses. There was no sign of a forced entry to the bungalow, so had Jean been killed by someone already within the household, or a friend or relative with a key? Or was it someone she knew and had invited in? Or perhaps it was someone who had tricked or forced their way in. This possibility might account for the fact that when Jean's home was later searched by police, various items including her handbag, bank cards and mobile telephone were found to be missing. Police already knew that there had been a number of dwelling house burglaries in the area during the preceding weeks. Was this simply a burglary that had gone badly wrong?

House-to-house enquiries were carried out in the immediate area, together with enquiries of local taxi companies, but no sightings of possible suspects emerged. Known house burglars were also interviewed and second hand property shops were checked; all to no avail.

Media appeals for witnesses and information were made. In fact, Steven and Tracy assisted by making personal appeals which were broadcasted on both radio and television. During one such media appeal Steven said, 'It has been absolute hell. It has been a nightmare for the last six months. I have tried to forget what I saw that night, but the memory is still there, day in, day out, no matter what you do. It's a vision I can't get out of my mind ... Somebody did this to my mum.'

Tracy said that until her mother's killer was found, there could be no closure. She went on, 'Every time the phone rings you think it's more news ... we're just keeping our fingers crossed and hope today somebody will come forward who knows something.' Unfortunately, no-one did.

But detectives had discovered more discrepancies in Steven's accounts. For example, a neighbour who had walked past the bungalow at 10.30pm that Wednesday night noticed that the television was off. However, Steven told police it was on when he arrived home. An audio recording of the '999' call made by Steven was listened to, but contrary to his assertions, no sound of him vomiting could be heard. Also, the door leading from the computer room that would allow him to access the kitchen was locked from the other side; so Steven could not have reached the dogs that way as he had claimed.

In themselves, they were minor discrepancies, but why had Steven apparently lied?

Detective Superintendent Wilson decided that Steven would now be treated as a suspect and he was invited to attend the local police station for a voluntary interview. This type of interview differs from a normal witness interview because Steven would not only be offered free and independent legal advice, he would also be formally cautioned before any questions were put to him and told that what he said may be used in evidence if he was later prosecuted.

Steven was questioned about a number of discrepancies in his earlier accounts to police and to others. He answered most of the questions put to him, but could not (or would not) give satisfactory explanations for all the discrepancies. Though puzzling, the discrepancies did not amount to evidence of his guilt, so no further action was taken against him and he was allowed to return home. But detectives had still not been able to eliminate him from the investigation.

In September 2003, a decision was taken that this and another unsolved murder investigation should be reviewed by the newly formed Major Crime Review Team. I took the lead on this review. (Peter Hamilton was already leading on another review which was successfully resolved.) By then the MIT had accumulated a significant amount of case material including statements, officers' reports, Actions (enquiries or tasks), interviews, other documents and computer records.

All this material had to be studied, a task that would take several months.

The review began with a briefing by the SIO and it was clear that detectives already knew that of all Jean's relatives, friends and acquaintances, including people she had met during her hospital stay, only Steven could not be satisfactorily eliminated from the murder investigation. It was important for the review to establish if Steven actually had a motive for killing his mother and if so, did he have the time and opportunity to commit the murder, dispose of any blood-stained clothing, the murder weapon and the missing property; then to establish an alibi for himself?

On the 9th September 2003, I was taken to the former crime scene by a member of the MIT. The bungalow had long since been restored to the family. This visit enabled me to see the layout of the bungalow and to understand the various witness accounts and the alleged discrepancies in some of Steven's statements.

We then drove to Steven's workplace and from there retraced the route Steven said he had taken on the night in question, i.e. from his workplace to his home, to Gary's mother's home, to the off-licence he stopped at en-route to Gary's home and back to Craigfield Avenue. Each stage of the journey was timed and the distances measured. That, and other information already obtained by detectives enabled me to reach certain conclusions.

Firstly, factory records showed that Steven had 'clocked off' at 6pm. He lived less than two miles from his workplace, a journey that took us only five minutes to drive; so Steven was likely to have arrived home around 6.05pm. Telephone records showed that Aunty May's telephone call was received at 6.11pm and had lasted for eight minutes.

Witnesses said that Steven had arrived at Gary's mother's home shortly after 8pm; The Weakest Link TV programme had only just started. Since she lived less than a mile from Steven's home, a journey time of two minutes, he had only to have left his home shortly before 8pm in order to have reached his first destination just after 8pm.

At 8.22pm Steven made a telephone call from Gary's mother's home, to Gary. Then, he drove to an off-licence in Key Road, Clacton, a two minutes, half mile journey.

Fortunately, these days there is so much technology surrounding any sale or purchase and this can aid an investigation. Closed circuit TV will often record a customer's arrival to and departure from a shop, credit card transactions are timed and dated, and most tills now produce timed and dated receipts. Loyalty or 'club cards' also leave accurate records of their use. Consequently, it was quite easy to establish that Steven had made his off-licence purchase at 8.36pm.

From the off-licence, Steven drove the remaining quarter of a mile journey to Gary's home, which took me less than one minute to complete.

The return journey from Gary's home to Steven's home was one and a half miles and took me six minutes in the 'rush hour'. It would have taken Steven far less time on the night of the murder as he was returning home after 10pm.

It was therefore clear that Steven had 'a window of opportunity' of approximately one hour and forty minutes, to commit the murder and to deal with the aftermath, i.e. from about 6.20pm, when Aunty May's telephone conversation with Jean had ended, to shortly before 8pm, the latest time he could have left home in time to arrive at Gary's mother's home just after 8pm.

True, he had given an account of the earlier part of his evening at home, the time he had spent with Jean prior to going out. But there were still a number of unanswered questions.

Why, for example, had Steven not had dinner with his mother like he usually did? In fact, there was no sign of Jean even having prepared a meal for them that evening. And why had Steven gone out that particular night when he usually stayed at home during the week; and how was it that on the only weekday evening he was away from home, that someone murdered Jean?

Furthermore, even if Steven had left home at 7.45pm as he claimed, why had it taken him over fifteen minutes to drive a two minute journey? Where else did he go and for what reason; and why had he not told police about that 'diversion'?

During the months that followed, I reviewed all the work already undertaken by detectives eventually coming to the same conclusion as they had; that the only person who could not be satisfactorily eliminated from Jean's murder was Steven Dicker.

However, what had surprised me was the fact that Steven Dicker appeared never to have been dealt with as one might have expected a murder suspect to be dealt with. He had initially been arrested on suspicion of murder, quickly de-arrested and for many weeks thereafter, had been treated as a witness. This was perhaps understandable because at that early stage detectives had no real evidence to treat him as a suspect. He could equally be a grieving son who was deserving of our support.

Nevertheless, there came a time when he was regarded as a suspect who needed to be re-interviewed about the inconsistencies in his statements. But even after being declared a suspect, he was not re-arrested. He simply attended his local police station for a voluntary interview. Steven had then been unable to satisfactorily explain the inconsistencies put to him, but was, nevertheless, allowed to leave.

It seemed to me that as Steven had not been satisfactory eliminated from the enquiry, he must still be a suspect for this brutal murder and should be dealt with accordingly. In short, he should be re-arrested and interviewed more robustly.

I discussed the conclusions of my review with the Director of Specialist Investigations, Detective Superintendent (later Detective Chief Superintendent) Simon Coxall, who requested a detailed report from me. I began that report with an examination of the circumstances surrounding the murder and considered various possibilities. I concluded that it was very unlikely that Jean would have allowed a stranger into her home that evening, especially after dark. Furthermore, there was no evidence to indicate that anyone had forcibly entered the bungalow and attacked her.

As previously stated, the hallway was L shaped with the main entrance at one end and the kitchen door, where her body was found, was at the other end. If someone had overpowered her at the front door, why was all the blood splattering found at the opposite end of this L shaped hallway?

No-one had seen or heard any unusual activity at the bungalow that evening, for example, any strangers either arriving or leaving, dogs barking, etc. If it was not a stranger then it had to be someone she knew, a relative or friend; maybe someone else with a key. But to the extent that it had been possible to do so, all Jean's relatives and friends had been eliminated from the enquiry.

The most likely explanation was, therefore, that Jean had been murdered by someone already in the bungalow, which only left Steven Dicker.

Interestingly, I have found that the answers to some mysteries may occasionally be found in the wisdom of fictional detectives like Sir Arthur Conan Doyle's Sherlock Holmes or Colin Dexter's creation, Detective Chief Inspector Morse. Holmes general advice to detectives was twofold and can be summarised thus. Firstly, the most obvious thing is probably the correct one, and secondly, if you have eliminated all other possibilities, whatever is left is probably what happened.

As previously stated, in this particular case relatives, friends and strangers had been eliminated from the enquiry and the most obvious explanation remaining was that Jean had been murdered by someone already in the bungalow, i.e. Steven Dicker. Steven had the opportunity to commit the crime and an earlier request by Gary to visit his (Gary's) mother, would provide him with the first part of his alibi.

There were also other things that might help Steven to escape justice. To start with, he was the only other person living there and they did not normally have visitors during the week. He could have been reasonably sure of not being disturbed as he dealt with the aftermath, i.e. cleaning himself up, changing his clothes, staging a burglary, etc.

And any forensic evidence could easily be accounted for since Steven actually lived there; and all three dogs knew him so were unlikely to create a fuss.

In terms of motive, Steven stood to inherit the bungalow; but he may not have been motivated by greed. It could equally be the case that for one reason or another, he simply lost his temper with Jean.

When considering that possibility, the level of violence used was particularly interesting. In 2000, Osterberg, et al, wrote about instances when violence is used that is far in excess of what is necessary to control or subdue a victim (as in this case).

Basically, the theory is that there is often a personal relationship between the victim and the killer which if subjected to stress may cause one to kill the other. If one can find the underlying cause, deductive reasoning may lead the investigator back to the one who may have been so motivated.

If Steven was the murderer then a personal relationship certainly existed between the victim and perpetrator. But what underlying stress was he suffering that was so great that it might have driven him to kill his mother?

During the year-long investigation detectives had discovered quite a lot about Steven from various relatives and friends. Having read all the statements and reports it was fairly easy for me to identify and to list the various aspects of his life that were probably causing him serious stress.

Firstly, Steven was not very happy to be living back with his mother; he had in effect replaced her late husband. Jean expected him to stay in every night to keep her company; also to run her around and to do all the jobs around the bungalow that her late husband used to do.

Secondly, he wanted to move out so as to be with his girlfriend; the situation was putting a strain on their relationship. But Steven was worried about how to tell his mother; and concerned about what she might do if he moved out leaving her alone again.

Steven was also worried about his job, especially since he had been unemployed for a long time before securing it. Overtime had recently been cut and he soon realised that his employment might not be as secure as he had once believed. Steven was amongst the most recent to be employed there, consequently, because of the 'lifo' practice (last in first out) he would probably be amongst the first to lose their jobs.

He also had concerns about his failing eyesight; concerns he had shared with others including Gary's mother.

Furthermore, Steven's car had recently required major repairs and as he was short of money he had to borrow from his mother in order to pay for those repairs.

Individually, all these problems were not serious; but one can imagine the cumulative effect they may have been having on Steven in January 2003. Emotionally he was probably a ticking 'time bomb', and it would not, perhaps, have taken much for him to explode.

A year into the investigation, we were at the stage where detectives had effectively explored and eliminated all other possible explanations for the murder, except that it had been committed by Steven.

I recommended that Steven should be arrested on suspicion of murder and that he should be questioned more rigorously. It was now time for him, rather than relatives and friends, to tell police about everything that was going on in his life in the run up to the murder, especially about the things that caused him stress. And if this had been an unpremeditated murder, what had happened that night to cause him to suddenly attack his mother?

Steven also needed to provide an even more detailed account of his movements during the evening of Jean's murder. What he had said thus far did not fit all the known facts, especially the timings he had provided.

Then there were still the other discrepancies in his accounts. For example, how had he gone through the door between the computer room and the kitchen when it had been locked from the other side?

It was not good enough for him simply to say that he could not explain this and the other discrepancies in his earlier accounts. He needed to be really pressed on It these matters.

Steven had also to be questioned about other possible motives or reasons for the murder. He was obviously in financial difficulties and knew he stood to inherit the bungalow. Could that have been his motive?

Furthermore, once Steven was in custody, key witnesses could also be re-interviewed. When they had earlier been seen by police, Steven was not in custody and they may have feared what he might do if, knowing or suspecting he was the killer, they co-operated with the police. He may also have said something significant to them after police had earlier interviewed him as a suspect.

On the 4th April 2004, Steven Dicker was arrested on suspicion of his mother's murder. He was booked into custody and then taken for interview. The usual formalities were completed and the questioning began.

Steven suddenly confessed to the murder of his mother. He then took detective out along the route he had taken immediately after the murder when disposing of the evidence, including his blood-stained clothing, the murder weapon and the items allegedly stolen from his mother, including her mobile telephone and handbag.

On the 5th April 2004, he was charged with murder and later put before the court where he was remanded in custody.

On the 21st December 2004, at Basildon Crown Court, Steven Dicker pleaded guilty to his mother's murder. The court was told by the prosecutor Peter Lodder QC (now a circuit judge), that Steven Dicker had hit his mother at least three times with a hammer. Nevertheless, he had the presence of mind to dispose of his blood-stained clothing and various items belonging to Jean, before setting up an alibi for himself.

He was remanded in custody for sentence.

Steven apologised to his sister Tracy and her family, '... for everything I have done.'

Speaking after the hearing Tracy said that her brother's admission had been a relief to the family and that the last year or so had been extremely difficult for them all. 'It's now approaching the time that we are able to move on and get our lives back to some sort of normality. Finally, mum can rest in peace.'

Detective Superintendent Gareth Wilson said that the investigation had been fraught with complications, partly because Steven Dicker had been a key witness and had made several appeals to catch the killer.

On the 31st January 2005, Steven Dicker returned to Basildon Crown Court before His Honour Judge Philip Clegg. The court was told that Steven had been banging a nail in the wall with a hammer, in order to hang a picture up. Jean began to criticise him and he hit her on the head at least three times, then stamped on her. He was sentenced to life imprisonment and ordered to serve a minimum of thirteen years before he could be considered for release.

The Judge then addressed Steven. 'I dare say that at times she could be demanding and difficult. It cannot be easy looking after someone who is deeply depressed. I am prepared to accept ... that you suddenly lost your temper when she criticised you over the manner in which you were attempting to knock a nail into the wall to hang a picture. But whatever your thought process may have been your reaction was horrific. She was scarcely recognisable after you had finished. And while your mother lay there, either dead or dying on the floor ... you did everything you could to make it look as if she had been the victim of a burglar or robber and that you had a watertight alibi.'

Speaking outside the court Tracy said that as far as she was concerned she no longer had a brother.

Detective Superintendent Wilson said, 'It's fair to say that if Steven had not admitted the murder we would not be here today. His confession came out of the blue during an interview ... he surprised us by stopping the interview and basically saying he wanted to plead guilty to murder.'

Whilst understanding the SIO's point of view, I think it failed to fully acknowledge the considerable work carried out by officers investigating and reviewing the murder over the fifteen month period leading up to Steven's arrest. By then the officers had eliminated all possible suspects from amongst Jean's relatives and friends; and had eliminated local criminals. They had identified various discrepancies in Steven Dicker's accounts and shown that he had both the opportunity and propensity to have committed this crime. Finally, investigators had also identified the various stresses acting on him which, whilst not excusing what he did, provided an explanation for his actions.

In short, the investigation had been brought to a stage where there was really only one possible explanation which was that Steven Dicker had killed his mother.

Steven Dicker's arrest in April 2004 must have come completely 'out of the blue' to him; and on first entering the interview room it must have been obvious to him from the maps displayed, the statements and other documents laid out before him, that the police had worked tirelessly on this investigation and were not just going to file it as 'unsolved'. If it had simply been the case that he wanted to confess the crime, he did not have to wait until police re-arrested him.

The SIO also later acknowledged the value in having an on-going unsolved investigation such as this one, independently reviewed and all officers involved in this investigation and review were commended by the Chief Constable.

Finally, I believe we sometimes under-estimate the effect that committing a murder has on some killers. Steven had to live with what he had done for more than a year and in some strange way it was probably quite a relief for him, when he was finally arrested and provided with the opportunity to admit his mother's murder.

I remember once interviewing a local so called 'hard man' named Danny, who had stabbed an innocent young man to death. The day before the killing, Danny had picked a fight with a man who was drinking in the same bar. Unfortunately for Danny, his would-be victim got the better of him. Danny decided to return to the pub next day to exact revenge.

This time he took a carving knife with him, but probably because he was under the influence of alcohol, he stabbed the wrong man who died shortly after.

Danny was later arrested and admitted the killing; but when he found out he had stabbed an innocent man, he broke down in tears.

Some killers cannot live with what they have done and commit suicide; others immediately give themselves up to the police. Those who do not will eventually confide in someone because they cannot bear the burden alone. Consequently there are individuals living amongst us who continue struggling on because they either committed a serious unsolved crime or they have important information about one. I would urge them to come forward.

Police have gained considerable experience in dealing with major crimes, especially unsolved 'Cold Cases'. Those who are still holding back should realise that there may never be a better time to come forward, if only so that the victims can be finally laid to rest.

CHAPTER 7
THE MURDER OF VIOLET DUNDERDALE

When a murder victim is found dead at home and within a secure setting, there are a limited number of possibilities. The murderer could be a member of the same household, a friend or relative with a key, or (albeit less likely) an unexpected caller that the victim invited into their home.

However, when the murder victim lives alone and is found dead in bed, in an allegedly insecure house, the range of suspects is much wider. Clearly it will not be someone who lives under the victim's roof; no one else does. Nor, if they were attacked whilst sleeping in bed, is it likely to be a caller invited in by the victim. Obviously the killer could still be a relative or friend; but then again it could be literally *anyone* who found the house insecure and crept inside.

These were the possibilities facing detectives investigating the murder of Violet Dunderdale. In July 1999, she was a seventy seven year-old widow living alone in a house in Archers Way, Galleywood, on the outskirts of Chelmsford. Her husband had died two years before, but she still had family living close by. Her son, Peter Dunderdale, lived less than a hundred yards away and living next door to him was his wife Patricia, known as 'Pat', and their thirty five year-old son Edward, known as 'Eddie'. The couple had two other sons, but they lived in Canada. In fact, Peter was visiting them at the time of Violet's murder.

Eddie was an unemployed Paranoid Schizophrenic who chain smoked. Local people later said that he was always scruffy in appearance and often appeared unwashed.

Violet was affectionately known as 'Nan' and after her death neighbours described her as a well-loved community figure who was always happy to stop and chat; and to share her homemade bread and cakes. Violet was also a smoker and enjoyed the occasional drink. In fact she would often join the rest of the family at the local Royal British Legion Social Club.

On Sunday 25th July 1999, Violet, Pat and Eddie went to a car boot sale where the two women purchased 100 Benson and Hedges cigarettes.

Later that evening they all went to the social club for a drink. After leaving the club, they had a cigarette in Pat's garden after which Pat walked Violet back to her own home. Pat only ever went as far as Violet's back garden before returning home. They had an arrangement that once she was safely inside her house, Violet would give Pat two rings on the telephone. That night was no different.

Pat was later to tell police that Eddie went to bed first and that she retired around 1am. Pat also told officers that she got up during the night and heard Eddie snoring in his bed. Pat also recalled that she finally went back to bed at 3am.

Pat then described how she was suddenly awoken by Eddie who told her that he had been to his Nan's house and that she was covered in blood. During the next few minutes, Pat telephoned the ambulance service (the '999' call was logged at 6.38am), her husband in Canada and a family friend, 'Tony'.

On his mother's instructions, Eddie returned to Violet's house to await the arrival of the ambulance. Soon he was joined by 'Tony' who noticed that Eddie was unusually clean and tidy in appearance, '... as though dressed for church'.

Together they entered the house where 'Tony' saw Violet dead in her bed. She had sustained severe head injuries; blood was splashed around the bedroom walls and ceiling. Clearly she had been attacked in bed, probably whilst sleeping. Paramedics attended and quickly confirmed that Violet was dead.

Police were immediately suspicious of Eddie. Why, for example, had he gone round his grandmother's house so early in the morning? The front door was also securely bolted and chained from the inside; and Violet always locked her back door. So how had the killer got into the house if not with a key, which Eddie had one of? Eddie was arrested on suspicion of murder and taken to Chelmsford Police Station.

A police surgeon was called to the scene and at 8.40am certified death. He estimated that Violet had been dead for about three hours, plus or minus three hours.

This meant that the attack could have occurred any time after 2.40am. Similarly, paramedics said that her body was still warm to the touch, indicating that she had probably not been dead very long.

A post mortem examination later established that the cause of death was multiple head injuries. There had been at least three blows to Violet's head and the pattern of blood staining and splattering on and around her body indicated that those blows had been inflicted whilst she was laying in her bed.

Violet's handbag containing £60 was lying on the bed and a later search of the house established that nothing of any value appeared to be missing; so theft did not appear to be the motive for her murder.

Officers carried out a preliminary search of the area immediately outside her house and found a ball-pein hammer lying discarded in a bed of nettles nearby. They noticed it had insulating tape around the handle and this unusual feature was later found to match other tools in Violet's home, tools that had once belonged to her late husband. They concluded that the hammer had probably come from Violet's home.

Forensic scientists examined the crime scene. Amongst other things, they found a shoeprint on the outside of Violet's bedroom door. In the kitchen sink they also found blood which was later found to match Violet's, plus a blood-stained hair which experts concluded had probably originated from Violet, Eddie or a maternal relative. They concluded that one possible explanation for the blood and hair being found in the sink was that the killer had tried to clean the murder weapon there, washing the blood-stained hair off the hammer in the process.

House-to-house enquiries were carried out and various neighbours told police what they had seen and heard. One had awoken at dawn (around 5.15am) and heard noises coming from Violet's house, including items being moved around; and finally, the back door slamming. Another heard a scream around 5.30am, but at the time thought it may have come from her television, which had been left on.

Then, around 5.50am, another neighbour saw someone running from the direction of Violet's house in the direction Eddie's home. But it was only a fleeting glance and that witness was unable to describe the person seen; in fact unable to even say if it was a man or a woman.

Having arrived at the police station, Eddie was searched and found to be in possession of some Benson and Hedges cigarettes. Had they come from his grandmother's house?

His clothing was seized to preserve any forensic evidence. It was later examined, but no blood was found thereon. However, scientists did find minute blood splattering on Eddie's trainers. The pattern of blood splattering indicated that the wearer of the trainer had been in close proximity to *a* person who was bleeding. Unfortunately, the blood spots were so tiny that they could not confirm, or otherwise, that it was actually Violet's blood.

Whilst being booked into custody, Eddie said he could hear voices, a not uncommon symptom of Schizophrenia. In view of this he was subjected to a psychological assessment and declared unfit to be detained in police custody and unfit to be interviewed. Eddie was sectioned under the Mental Health Act and taken to a secure mental health unit. In fact, he remained in secure accommodation for the next few years.

Meanwhile, detectives attended Eddie's home and found his clothing in the washing machine, which was by then on the spin cycle. Had he gone home after committing the murder, washed himself and changed his blood-stained clothing before the emergency services had been called? If so this would explain why this usually scruffy individual had later appeared to be dressed as though for church.

Over time, Eddie gave various accounts of the events that led to him discovering his grandmother's body. He told one officer that he checked his grandmother every morning, using a back door key to get in. Eddie said he often had breakfast and a cigarette with her, although another relative disputed this saying that Eddie would never go round to his grandmother's house that early in the morning.

Eddie told his mother that he had gone for a walk and had noticed lights on in his grandmother's house and that was why he had gone inside.

On a different occasion, Eddie told his father that he had gone to his Nan's to have a cigarette. He said he did not know how long he had stayed with her and could not remember if he locked the back door when he finally left her house. Eddie later repeated this account in a statement written in hospital, observing that if he had failed to lock up then *anyone* could have gained entry to the house after he left.

Detectives suspected that he was adopting that line because how else could anyone have entered a secure house without making a forced entry? But it would be difficult for detectives to either prove or disprove what Eddie was now saying.

Investigators were also troubled by the fact that there had been some attempt to clean up the crime scene after the murder. Would Eddie have had the presence of mind to clean the murder weapon before dumping it; then to wash himself and his clothing, before raising the alarm?

Or did he receive help?

They knew that if he ever needed help, his mother was the person he would normally turn to; consequently both Eddie and his mother would have to be formally interviewed about their movements and actions that morning.

Having completed their initial enquiries, detectives concluded that Eddie was their number one suspect; but they would have to wait until his mental health improved before they could formally interview him.

In February 2000, doctors considered Eddie fit to be interviewed and in due course both he and his mother were formally interviewed. Both exercised their right not to answer the questions put to them.

A file of evidence was considered by the Crown Prosecution Service (CPS) who decided that there was insufficient evidence to charge either of them in connection with Violet Dunderdale's death. No further action was taken against them.

No other suspects were identified, so the investigation wound down. Meanwhile, Eddie continued to receive in-patient treatment of his illness.

In June 2000, an Inquest was held into Violet's death. The Coroner recorded a verdict of Unlawful Killing.

In 2001, Eddie's parents went to Canada to visit their sons and grandchildren. Unfortunately, whilst there, Pat developed a serious heart condition and was unable to return to the United Kingdom.

By 2005, Eddie's mental health had improved to the extent that he was released from the secure unit and went to live in the Colchester area under the supervision of community mental health professionals. Then, rather worryingly, the local police began receiving reports about Eddie's allegedly strange behaviour in public places. Whilst this was not necessarily criminal, it was causing them some concern.

In March 2005, a multi-agency case conference was convened and I was one of those in attendance. The matters discussed were confidential and cannot be disclosed. Nevertheless, I returned to police headquarters with serious concerns about the emerging situation. On the face of it, we were dealing with a Paranoid Schizophrenic who was the main if not the only suspect for the violent murder of his grandmother; and he was back in the community and allegedly acting strangely.

An urgent 'Cold Case' review of the Violet Dunderdale murder was required if only try to confirm, or otherwise, Eddie's involvement in his grandmother's murder.

I retrieved the case papers and various items seized during the original investigation, including Eddie's trainers. I then spent several weeks re-examining the original investigation, studying all the statements, reports and other documents; and reviewing the exhibits that had been seized back in 1999. Having completed the review I made a number of recommendations, including one for a forensic re-examination of Eddie's trainers.

My hope was that as the science of DNA had progressed, the tiny bloodstains originally found on the trainers might now yield a DNA profile that would enable us to identify exactly whose blood it was. Eddie's trainers were examined once again and this time a mixed DNA profile was developed, i.e. a profile of more than one person. The major component of this mixed DNA profile matched Violet Dunderdale's DNA profile. The remainder of the mixed DNA profile originated from two other people. One was Eddie, which was not perhaps surprising as they were his trainers and would likely have traces of his DNA, etc., thereon. The remainder of the mixed profile was eventually matched to one of the scientists involved in the scientific examination!

Furthermore, scientists were now able to confirm that the pattern of blood-staining on the trainers indicated that the wearer of the shoe, i.e. Eddie, must have been present when Violet had been attacked. Those findings, together with all the other circumstantial evidence, confirmed our suspicions that Eddie had been directly involved in his grandmother's murder.

On the 18th July 2005, detectives from Stanway Major Investigations Team, led by Detective Superintendent (later Temporary Assistant Chief Constable) Colin Steele, were briefed by me and took over the re-investigation. As in the Norah Trott case, they would need to trace and re-interview the original witnesses and commission further forensic work.

As a result of all their work, on the 4th October 2005, Edward Dunderdale was once again arrested on suspicion of murder. Whilst in custody he was interviewed, but again made no admissions. A further file of evidence had then to be considered by the CPS, so Eddie was technically released on police bail. By then his mental health had been further assessed and he was now in a semi-secure mental health unit.

On the 1st March 2006, Edward Dunderdale was arrested and charged with the murder of Violet Dunderdale. The next day he was remanded in custody to await trial.

On the 25th June 2007, at Basildon Crown Court, Edward Dunderdale's trial began before His Honour Judge Christopher Ball QC. He pleaded not guilty to his grandmother's murder.

However, on the third day the trial was halted. The prosecution was about to introduce evidence showing that the footprint on Violet's bedroom door had probably been left by one of Eddie's trainers, perhaps as he kicked it open. After adjourning the case Judge Ball dismissed the jury and ordered that the charge be put to Edward Dunderdale once more. This time he pleaded guilty to Manslaughter on the grounds of Diminished Responsibility.

Diminished responsibility is one of three special defences which exist solely for the offence of murder. Where the defence of diminished responsibility is successfully advanced it basically reduces a 'Murder' conviction (carrying an automatic sentence of life imprisonment) to 'Manslaughter', where the actual sentence is decided by the trial judge. It does not completely absolve the defendant from liability, but explains why he or she carried out the killing.

What has to be shown when 'Manslaughter' has been admitted is firstly, that the accused suffered from an abnormality of the mind caused by a recognised medical condition (in this case Schizophrenia). Next, that the abnormality provides an explanation for their acts or omissions in being party to the killing. Thirdly, that the condition substantially impaired their mental ability to understand the nature of their behaviour or to form a rational judgement or to exercise self control.

The following week, Judge Ball ordered that Edward Dunderdale be detained indefinitely under the Mental Health Act, in a secure unit at Runwell Hospital. His Honour acknowledged that Eddie had been suffering a severe psychiatric illness at the time of the murder.

He said, 'It is plain to everyone that you were fond of your grandmother and loved her dearly and helped her enormously. Something plainly terrible happened that night to make you attack her in the way you did. It can only be attributed to the long standing mental illness you suffer. You pleaded guilty to manslaughter on the grounds of diminished responsibility, and it is possible for me to pass a sentence which is designed to help you through your illness as far as possible, as well as ensure the safety of the public.'

Speaking after the trial, Detective Superintendent Steele said, 'Violet Dunderdale was an elderly grandmother who did not deserve to have her life cut short in such tragic and violent circumstances. We are delighted to see that justice has finally been done.'

I was also delighted with the result which would probably not have been achieved had Essex Police not invested in a Major Crime Review Team. The review, plus the subsequent re-investigation and conviction, not only bought Violet's killer to justice, but, in my view, has protected the people of Essex from the risk that Eddie may still have posed following his earlier release.

Finally, in November 2011, Eddie's father Peter told a local newspaper that his son had told him during recent visits, that he had contacted a firm of London solicitors and that an appeal (against his conviction) was being prepared.

By the time of my retirement (in 2014), I had not been formally notified of any such appeal.

CHAPTER 8
'NO BODY' MURDERS

'Cold Cases' cannot always be resolved; but further investigation can often move a case forward, thus improving the chances of it one day being solved.

Reviews are especially important in cases, like that of Dinah McNicol, where a person disappeared in suspicious circumstances and is believed to have been murdered, but their body cannot be found. These are known within the police service as 'No Body' Murderers. If such cases can be solved, there is a chance that the body can be recovered and returned to the family for a decent burial.

Over the years there have been a number of 'No Body Murder' cases in Essex. They include the strange disappearance of a Filipina woman, China Rose Sims, who went missing from Southend-on-Sea in February 1993. At the time, Mrs Sims was married to an ex-Metropolitan Police officer, David Sims. She vanished shortly after telling her sister Joy, that her husband was becoming increasingly violent towards her. Joy recalled her sister saying that he (David Sims) told her he was going to get someone to kill her, because it would be '... cheaper than getting a divorce.'

Soon after that conversation with her sister, China Rose went missing. Shortly after that, David also disappeared; and neither has been seen or heard of since.

Then there is the case of Sandra Gant who went missing from Clacton-on-Sea in 2003. Sandra, then forty eight years-old, was a married woman with four grown up children. However, when her marriage broke down after twenty years she became depressed and started drinking heavily. Sandra became a familiar sight in and around Clacton town centre.

Although now living alone in a flat in Wellesley Road, Clacton, Sandra still kept in close contact with her children, especially her youngest daughter whom she met regularly every Thursday week. In fact they were next due to meet on the 20th November 2003, but Sandra failed to keep the appointment.

Enquiries revealed that on the 15th November 2003, Sandra visited a soup kitchen where she joined a couple of friends and a man she had not previously met. He invited all three back to his flat for a drink. They later told police that around 10pm that evening, Sandra left the flat on her own intending to make her way home. She has not been seen or heard of since.

It is not known if Sandra ever left the flat and if she did, if she ever arrived home. But one of her daughters later checked her mother's flat to find the heater on; also, a number of items that Sandra would normally have with her were still in the flat. These included two necklaces and her tobacco tin. Had Sandra actually arrived back home that night and gone missing from there?

What began as a routine missing person's investigation soon became a 'No Body' murder investigation led by Detective Superintendent Gareth Wilson of Stanway Major Investigations Team. In due course a number of people were arrested and interviewed, but they denied all knowledge of her disappearance and were released on police bail. No further action was subsequently taken against any of them.

Sandra's family is convinced that she has been murdered and they have made many media appeals for information.

On the seventh anniversary of Sandra's disappearance, a further appeal for information was made by the newly appointed Senior Investigating Officer, Detective Chief Inspector Godfrey O'Toole. He said, 'We know there are people living in Clacton who have crucial information on Sandra's last moments and where she is now. Someone holds the key to unlocking the mystery surrounding her disappearance and presumed death.'

Sandra's daughter Carrie said, 'We need to find our mum to bring her home and lay her to rest, knowing she is no longer lost and alone will release us of our nightmare and finally allow us to grieve in peace with our memories.'

Then there is the case of Nicola Ray. In May 2000, Nicola was a twenty nine year-old unemployed barmaid and mother of two, living with her fiancé Tim, in his house in Pitsea on the outskirts of Basildon.

They were due to marry that summer.

Nicola's eldest daughter Joedy, then aged eleven, lived with Nicola and Tim; and Nicola's youngest daughter Stevie, then aged seven, lived with her natural father. Tim worked at one of Ford Motor's sites in Essex.

Monday 1st May 2000, was a Bank Holiday and all three, Tim, Nicola and Joedy, got up intending to go to Southend-on-Sea for the day. But during their journey Nicola changed her mind and decided instead to go out for a drink with her close friend, Loretta Kenny. Tim decided to visit his parents.

Nicola took Joedy to Loretta's house in nearby Devlins, where she played with Loretta's daughter. Their mothers, meanwhile, got ready to go out and then went off to the Basildon town centre for a drink in the Moon in the Square public house. Having spent the evening socialising, Nicola and Loretta returned to Loretta's home around midnight.

Nicola then telephoned Tim to let him know that she would be staying at Loretta's for the night. But shortly after making that call, Nicola changed her mind and rang Tim back to let him know that she was, after all, coming home. Nicola told Tim that she would start walking home and Tim said he would meet her at the local shops from where they would walk home together. Apart from Tim, Loretta was the last person known to have seen Nicola alive.

When later seen by police, Tim confirmed that he had indeed met Nicola at the shops and had walked home with her. He told officers that he then went to bed as he had to work the next day. According to Tim, Nicola was asleep when he went off to work the following morning, but not at home when he returned from work; and she did not come home that day. It was arranged that Joedy would stay with Loretta until Nicola's return.

Tim later told police that he went to work the following day (Wednesday 3rd May) and on returning home later that afternoon, he found that some of Nicola's personal property was missing. He later told police that he had assumed that Nicola had returned home whilst he was at work and that she had now moved out for good.

At that time he did not seem overly concerned about Nicola's disappearance as he did not report it to the police.

A couple of days later Tim cancelled the wedding and honeymoon.

At first sight, his actions may appear odd, but he was probably upset and annoyed with Nicola for a number of reasons. Firstly, it must have appeared to him that Nicola had preferred to spend the Bank Holiday out drinking with her friend, rather than with him. She had then telephoned him late at night (knowing he had to be up for work early next morning) to say she was staying at Loretta's house. Then, shortly after, she rang him again, this time to say that she had changed her mind and was about to start walking home. Due to the lateness of the hour he probably felt obliged to meet her. Then Nicola moved out the next day without even speaking to him.

If what Tim told police was true, he could be forgiven for concluding that he and Nicola had no real future together; and that would perhaps explain why he displayed little interest in her whereabouts and cancelled the wedding and honeymoon.

In fact, Nicola's disappearance was not reported to the police for a couple of weeks, and then only after a member of Nicola's family had returned from holiday and was unable to contact her.

A routine missing person's investigation commenced. Nicola's home was searched and some of her clothing found to be missing. But despite numerous enquiries and media appeals, officers failed to locate her. By then concerns for Nicola's safety and well-being were beginning to emerge. Speaking at the time, Miss Kenny said of Nicola, 'She loved her kids and it would take something serious for her not to contact them.'

The case was then referred to the Rayleigh Major Investigations Team led by Detective Superintendent (later Chief Superintendent) Dick Madden. Further enquiries were carried out by the team and in February 2001, Tim, then thirty eight years-old, was arrested on suspicion of murder. His house was again searched, as indeed were a number of other locations in the area; however, Nicola was not found.

Tim was subsequently released from custody and no further action was taken against him.

Many years later, as the case approached its tenth anniversary, a decision was taken to review the Nicola Ray investigation. I recovered all the case papers and other records and during the next few months studied all this material. One of the most important discoveries made was that despite officers' best efforts, they had not been able to obtain a DNA profile of Nicola. It was crucial that we again try to obtain this since her body (or parts thereof) may not be discovered for many years and without her DNA profile it would be very difficult to quickly identify her. A great deal of work was carried out in order to develop her DNA profile, but the outcome cannot yet be revealed for operational reasons.

The review also concluded, amongst other things, that further house-to-house enquiries should be carried out. No replies had been received at a number of the homes visited during the original investigation. Important witness information may therefore have been missed.

This situation was not unusual. Police will normally visit homes in the vicinity of an incident and will return several times if no one is home. If they are unable to get a reply after several attempts, letters requesting contact will be delivered. Unfortunately, some occupants still fail to make contact.

The re-investigation was passed to the Brentwood Major Investigations Team then led by Detective Superintendent Tracy Hawkings, and Operation Tattoo was launched.

In April 2010, police, forensic and other experts returned to Nicola's former home where they conducted a further forensic search of the property. In particular, they were looking for signs of any soil disturbance below ground level, but nothing of any significance was found. Nevertheless, the resumed house-to-house enquiries did secure further important witness evidence.

For a second time, Tim was arrested on suspicion of murder, but once again he was again released without charge.

There is still no evidence to show that Tim was in any way responsible for Nicola's disappearance.

I do not believe Nicola disappeared voluntarily. When she left home Nicola was only months away from her wedding and honeymoon. For her it was to be a new start in life. She had two girls whom she loved; and a family who loved her. Nicola also suffered a medical condition that required regular monitoring and treatment; and she was not in a position to support herself financially, especially without her benefits. They have not been claimed since she disappeared.

In all probability Nicola is dead and the case will be reviewed again in due course. It is to be hoped that one day someone will find the courage to come forward with information that will enable the police to recover Nicola's body and return it to her family.

They, like the families of China Rose Sims and Sandra Gant, should not have to go through life without being able to finally lay them to rest.

CHAPTER 9
RAPE AND SERIOUS SEXUAL ASSAULT

Though centuries old, the offence of rape and the attitudes of some police officers dealing with rape victims, have undergone significant changes over a relatively short period of time. For example, when I first became a detective, rape was quite simply, 'Unlawful sexual intercourse (i.e. intercourse outside the bonds of marriage) with a female, by force, fear or fraud.' So much has changed since then; and quite rightly so.

Firstly, a woman is no longer regarded a being the property of her husband. He can now be convicted of raping her if he has sexual intercourse with her against her will.

Secondly, rape can also be committed against a male whereas previously only females could be the victims of rape.

Furthermore, a number of the more serious sexual assault, not previously amounting to rape, will now be treated just as seriously as rape if the acts involve some kind of penetration.

There was also a time when some officers (including me) approached rape investigations with a degree of scepticism unless there was clear evidence from the outset that rape had occurred. Unfortunately, this approach sometimes influenced the way we treated rape victims. In effect, rape victims had almost to prove they had been raped, before their case would be fully investigated. As a result, some withdrew their allegations, not because they were untrue, but because they could not handle such unsympathetic treatment.

Some officers (including me) felt they could justify their approach (if ever it could be justified) on the basis that if the victim could not cope with robust, often insensitive, questioning by the police, they would not survive the prosecution process. Once in court their dress, behaviour, character and morals would become the central issues; and the rape itself would be almost incidental. This was because the law permitted defence counsel to probe areas of the victim's personal life which would not be permitted today.

Looking back, I regret those occasions when I was not more sympathetic and supportive of some of the victims I came into contact with. But I hope that my later work on unsolved 'Cold Case' rapes and in improving modern rape and serious sexual assault investigations has at least, in part, made up for this.

During the past decade or so, the police service has had to 'wake up' to the fact that they sometimes provided a very poor service to victims of rape and other serious sexual assaults; just as it has had to acknowledge that on too many occasions their response to victims of domestic abuse was equally wanting.

Mistakes are still made, but overall, police officers (not just detectives) are now better trained and equipped to respond to allegations of rape and serious sexual assault. There is now a presumption that allegations of rape are genuine and will be treated as such, unless there is clear evidence from the outset that the alleged attack did not occur. For example, a victim may claim she was attacked at a particular time and location, but closed circuit TV (CCTV) actually proves otherwise.

Most police forces take their responsibilities in this area so seriously that specialist teams have been set up. In Essex, for example, Sexual Offences Investigations Teams (SOIT's) have been established around the county. Furthermore, once a rape allegation has been made, an officer not below the rank of Detective Inspector will immediately assume responsibility for the investigation.

If the victim is a child who has been assaulted within a family setting, or is an adult survivors of sexual abuse committed when they were children, the investigation will be undertaken by specially trained officers from the Child Abuse Investigations Team (CAIT).

Officers responding to a report of rape will firstly ensure that the victim is safe; and once their safety has been ensured, the officers will take early action to prevent the loss of any forensic evidence. Previously, rape victims may have had to wait several hours to see the Police Surgeon before they could have a drink or use the toilet. However, officers now use Early Evidence Kits to secure any forensic evidence.

These kits contain swabs, saliva and urine collection containers; and once any samples have been taken the victim can have a drink or use the toilet with minimal risk of any loss of forensic evidence.

Unless the attack occurred more than a week or so before, the victim will then be taken to a Sexual Assault Referral Centre (SARC) which is often housed within a hospital setting. Once there, they will be met by a specially trained officer who will support them and assist the Police Surgeon, now more commonly known as a Forensic Medical Examiner (FME).

In Essex, these specialist officers are known as Sexual Offences Trained Officers (SOTO's). They will obtain an early account of the attack and may later take the victim's witness statement. The SOTO will often become one the main points of contact with the victim during the on-going investigation.

At the SARC, the victim will undergo a forensic medical examination during which various samples are taken. Usefully, the SARC is also a 'one stop shop' where the victim can be offered further support, counselling and any necessary medical advice or treatment. They will then be interviewed in a purpose built interview suite. Any clothing worn at the time of the attack, or other items such as bedding, will be recovered for forensic examination.

Detectives will conduct a thorough investigation during which they will liaise with the Crown Prosecution Service (CPS) which also has its own rape specialist lawyers. Joint Police / CPS case building provides the best chance of securing a conviction.

For the purposes of investigation, rapes are classified according to the particular circumstances of the case; and the resulting investigations will be carried out by the most appropriate specialist teams. The rapes may be 'acquaintance rapes', where the victims and suspects are known to each other; 'child sexual abuse'; or 'domestic rape', committed by the victim's partner, ex-partner or other family member, including the extended family.

The rape categories also included 'drug or alcohol assisted rapes', where substances have been given to victims in order to secure compliance; and 'multiple-offender rapes', which, as the name implies, involves the rape of a victim by more than one person. In most of these cases victims and offenders are known to each other so identifying the person responsible is not usually a problem.

The final category of rape is that of 'Stranger Rape', which involves attacks on victims by suspects who are unknown to each other, albeit that their 'paths' may have previously crossed. Of all sexual predators, the 'Stranger Rapist' is the most feared. The idea of being dragged into an alleyway or field and raped by a complete stranger horrifies victims, especially women; but thankfully such cases are relatively rare.

In reality, all rapes are serious and the fact that the victim may know the attacker does not really make the experience any more bearable. In some ways it makes it worse, as it invariably results in a significant breach of trust and the end of a relationship.

Being able to categorise the type of attack assists investigators as there are specific lines of enquiry that can be followed for each category; and considerable effort is now expended in bringing rapists to justice.

But it is also an unfortunate fact of life that some allegations of rape are false. This can be problematic as an allegation of rape is easy to make, hard to prove; but even harder to disprove. But it is important that false rape allegations are properly dealt with.

The Court of Appeal made their views clear in the case of Regina v Carrington-Jones (16.10.2007). *'Their Lordships said that although no one doubted that victims of rape had to be treated with every possible consideration by the criminal justice system, a false allegation could have dreadful consequences for an innocent man who had not perpetrated the crime. Also, every occasion of a proved false allegation had an insidious effect on public confidence in the truth of genuine complaints, sometimes allowing doubt to creep in where none should exist.'*

Although every effort is made to resolve rapes, especially the more difficult 'Stranger Rapes', this is not always possible. Some cases eventually have to be 'shelved' pending further information or evidence. This is when 'Cold Case' reviews of unsolved 'Stranger Rape' investigations come into their own.

Essex Police, like most other forces across the United Kingdom, has made considerable progress with such investigations. Consequently, around the country there are scores of rapists who are now in prison despite thinking they had got away with their crimes; still others will join them in due course.

Former rape victims will not always be aware that their case is being reviewed. This is because we recognise the distress that may be caused if police routinely contacted them whenever a review was underway. It is better to re-establish contact with a victim once detectives are reasonably sure they have identified the attacker.

Careful consideration is also given as to how any such contact may be re-established. In many cases the victim will have tried to put the matter behind them and may not have told others what had happened to them many years before.

Also, as with all 'Cold Cases', we do not want to raise hopes or expectations unnecessarily, especially in those cases where the review concludes that there is nothing that can be done, *at this moment in time,* to progress a particular investigation. Nevertheless, victims and / or relatives can be assured that no unsolved murder or 'Stranger Rape' is permanently filed. And just because they may have heard nothing years after the event, it does not necessarily mean that the investigation is dormant.

Unfortunately resolving such crimes it is not always as quick or as easy as the media sometimes portrays. Many problems are encountered along the way. The victim of a 'Stranger Rape', for example, may have since died, or perhaps it is the attacker who has since died. But even if the attacker is possibly dead, should we not still re-investigate in order to at least bring some form of closure to the victim and / or their family?

If nothing else they will know that the person responsible will never again harm them, or anyone else.

Some 'Cold Case' rape victims are not willing to co-operate with a review or re-investigation; they have long since put the incident behind them; or at least, have tried to. And whilst they would dearly love to see the rapist punished, they do not feel able to re-live their ordeal again, especially in court.

Police always take the victim's views into account, but we have an overriding duty to identify the attacker and to prosecute them if other supporting evidence can be found. This is because the attacker may have committed other crimes for which they have not yet been punished. Also, they may still pose a threat to the public, since many offend throughout their whole lifetime.

Often a DNA profile of the attacker will be developed, but the offender may not be identified simply because his DNA profile has never been obtained and loaded onto the National DNA Database (NDNAD). So how can the science of DNA be used to finally identify him?

More unusually, the offender may be one of identical twins. Both will have exactly the same DNA profile, so how can detectives determine which twin actually carried out the attack?

A number of Essex 'Cold Case' rape investigations have been reviewed and some have resulting in convictions (see next chapter). Interestingly, the outcomes of others were not always as expected.

On the evening of Friday 2nd November 1990, 'Jane' (not her real name) left her Basildon home to walk the short distance to her local social club. She was a confident, middle aged woman who lived alone, and though divorced, 'Jane' was still on good terms with her ex-husband. 'Jane' spent the evening socialising, before leaving the club to go home. There were few people out and about as 'Jane' walked home; however, she knew the area and her route home was well-lit

As she neared home, 'Jane' took a short cut, clambering over some low railings and onto the path that would eventually lead to her front door. It was then that a man, who she did not recognise, engaged her in conversation.

'Jane' tried to ignore him, but he persisted and she felt a sense of relief as she arrived home. But, as she turned her front door key in the lock, the man pushed his way into her house where he raped her before escaping into the night.

'Jane' then did all the right things. She immediately telephoned her ex-husband and two close friends, telling them what had just happened. The police were also informed and a rape investigation commenced. 'Jane' was medically examined and various swabs obtained for forensic examination; but despite extensive enquiries, the rapist was not identified.

In 2006, this rape investigation was one of a number of 'Cold Cases' that the Review Team looked at. A DNA profile of the rapist was subsequently developed from semen recovered from one of 'Jane's' internal vaginal swabs. It matched a petty criminal who was now living in Hampshire.

The re-investigation was passed to Harlow Major Investigations Team, led by Detective Superintendent Tim Wills. They made further enquiries which, sadly, revealed that 'Jane' had since died. Although her death could not be directly linked to the rape, those who knew her were later to tell police that she never really recovered from the attack.

The death of a rape victim does not automatically mean that a prosecution cannot be undertaken; but it often makes it more difficult to convict an offender.

Background enquiries into the suspect revealed that he had once worked in the Basildon area, and detectives later identified one of his relatives who lived not far from 'Jane' and with whom he had occasionally stayed.

The original witnesses were traced and re-interviewed; all said they would support a prosecution.

In due course, the suspect was arrested and interviewed by Essex Police detectives at a police station in Hampshire. He readily admitted that sexual intercourse had taken place between 'Jane' and himself. He explained to detectives that he had met 'Jane' several weeks before the night in question and had bumped into her again that Friday night.

They allegedly got chatting again and ended up having sex together; all with her consent. This account placed detectives in a very difficult position since 'Jane' was dead and they could neither prove nor disprove, the suspect's story. Reluctantly, the Senior Investigating Officer decided that no further action could be taken against the suspect and although this was a disappointing result, at least the suspect was now 'on the police radar' as a suspected sex offender.

The matter would have ended there, but following the suspect's arrest on suspicion of rape, his step-sister came forward alleging that when she was younger, he had sexually abused her as well. He was arrested by Hampshire detectives, interviewed about this historic allegation and a report was submitted to the Crown Prosecution Service (CPS) for consideration of a prosecution.

Full details of 'Jane's' allegation of rape and what the suspect had said about it when interviewed by Essex detectives, were forwarded to Hampshire CPS so they could consider prosecuting both cases together. Alternatively, the CPS could consider the Basildon attack as possible 'bad character' evidence.

'Bad character' evidence in criminal proceedings means 'evidence of or a disposition towards misconduct (section 99 Criminal Justice Act 2003). 'Misconduct' means the commission of an offence or other 'reprehensible conduct' (section 112 Criminal Justice Act 2003.) For example, if a person committed a sexual assault and was later charged with another sexual assault, his previous actions could be used at his new trial, as evidence to show that he had a propensity to commit sexual assaults.

Perhaps surprisingly, the suspect who had allegedly attacked 'Jane', appeared at Crown Court and pleaded guilty to the indecent assault on his step-sister, a plea that was accepted by the CPS. He received a prison sentence which was suspended for 12 months. He was also made the subject of a Sex Offender's Notice for seven years and of a Restraining Order. I have not named him or provided any other personal details about him in order protect his victim(s) and family members.

Although he was never convicted of the rape allegedly committed on 'Jane', the 'Cold Case' review and the subsequent re-investigation had resulted in his conviction and punishment for an offence that might have otherwise remained secret.

In short, if he had not had sex with 'Jane' (with or without her consent) and then been identified as a suspect for that incident, his step-sister may never have come forward. As a result of this 'Cold Case' review, his step-sister can now draw a line under what he did to her, and he is now a convicted sex offender whose on-going behaviour will be monitored by the police and other agencies.

Another unusual case concerned the rape of a thirty five year-old care assistant attacked whilst walking in Westcliff-on-Sea, in 1992. It was early evening on Tuesday 27th October, and 'Claire' (not her real name) was walking to work along The Leas, just off the sea front. Suddenly, a clean shaven, but scruffily dressed man who she did not know, grabbed hold of her, dragging her into the foyer of a nearby block of flats. Despite 'Claire' struggling, the man pulled down her jeans and knickers before raping her. He then ran off.

'Claire' was very upset by what happened, but did not contact the police until the following day, and then only after her husband had persuaded her to do so. She was medically examined and made a statement outlining what had occurred. However, 'Claire' had been so traumatised by the attack that she felt unable to support the investigation. Nevertheless, detectives knew it was important to try to identify the attacker and so continued their investigation.

Forensic scientist found traces of semen on a number of internal and external swabs, but were only able to develop a part DNA profile of the attacker, who despite their enquiries, was not identified.

In 2006, the investigation was the subject of a 'Cold Case' review, which included further forensic work. As a result of that work a full DNA profile of the suspect was developed the following year. But when this was searched on the National DNA Database, it was found to match two men!

Further enquiries revealed that the reason for this was they were identical twins; and identical twins develop from the same egg.

The re-investigation was passed to Brentwood Major Investigations Team, then led by Detective Superintendent John Quinton. Both men's backgrounds were thoroughly researched and it was soon discovered that one had since died. Both men were known to the police, indeed one had been convicted of sexually motivated crimes whilst the other man's convictions did not include sex crimes. This did not necessarily mean that the former had committed the rape, although he seemed to be the more likely candidate.

Detectives checked police and other records to see what both men were doing on the 27th October 1992. Hopefully, one of them would have been in prison or in police custody; or perhaps they were visiting a Probation Officer, etc., and so could be eliminated from the re-investigation. Maybe one was on holiday, at work or in hospital, in fact anywhere that would have made it impossible for him to have been the rapist. Or perhaps one of them had a full beard on the 28th October 1992, and this would also rule him out.

Detectives needed to act quickly. The surviving twin was in prison, but was soon to be released; and if he was the rapist they did not want him back on the streets of Essex. Consequently, immediately upon his release from prison, the suspect was arrested and interviewed. He did not admit the attack so was released on police bail pending the outcome of further enquiries.

'Claire' was traced and updated with the results of the 'Cold Case' review. Unfortunately, she still felt unable to support the investigation and her views had to be taken into account. Nevertheless, as previously stated, police have always to consider the wider public interest and if sufficient evidence existed, even without the victim's evidence, the prosecution of a 'Stranger Rapist' would always be in the public interest.

Unfortunately, the investigation was unexpectedly halted when the second suspect died suddenly whilst out on bail. In some ways, this was probably the best outcome.

'Claire' would not now feel under any obligation to give evidence and as the rapist had been narrowed down to one of two men, both of whom were now dead, 'Claire' would no longer fear a further attack by him. And Essex is now a safer place for all women.

Another, perhaps not so cold 'Cold Case' rape review was also satisfactorily resolved.

One Saturday evening in September 2006, 'Tracy' (not her real name) went to a discothèque just off the Southend sea front. Shortly after midnight, she stepped outside to get a breath of fresh air. Suddenly she was allegedly 'frog-marched' across the road by a group of six young men and forced into some public toilets. Once inside they tore some of her clothing off and one-by-one raped and buggered her as she screamed for help. One also bit her. 'Tracy' then watched as they left the toilets and drove off in a car.

The attack was quickly reported to the police and a rape investigation was launched. 'Tracy' was medically examined and various samples taken for forensic examination. Initial enquiries failed to identify her alleged attackers.

A few days later 'Tracy' contacted the police saying that she was no longer willing to support an investigation and made a statement requesting no further action. However, she did not withdraw her allegations. Despite this development, the allegations were so serious that they still had to be investigated, with or without 'Tracy's' help. But despite their best efforts, detectives were unable to either prove or disprove what she had said.

The investigation was re-examined by the Review Team and a number of things were discovered. Firstly, it was found that 'Tracy' had made a several allegations during the previous couple of years. Most of those allegations seemed to involve accostings or assaults upon her by unidentified men. Could she really be that unlucky? But this is always a difficult area because although she has made similar unproven allegations in the past, it did not mean that she was lying on this latest occasion.

Next, there had been no other sightings of a group of men at the relevant time, either in or around the toilets. In particular, a bouncer on duty directly opposite the toilet block had not seen or heard anything untoward. Closed circuit TV recordings were studied and there was no sign of the car in which the group had allegedly escaped. Furthermore, 'Tracy' had raised the alarm immediately after the alleged attack, speaking to a number of passers-by and to various police officers called to the scene. She had given all of them descriptions of her attackers. However, when all these descriptions were collated and compared, significant differences were noted.

The medical evidence was also reviewed and 'Tracy's' clothing examined. No evidence of her having been violently attacked by up to six men, or of her having been bitten, was found.

A number of recommendations were made to the detectives investigating this attack the most important of which was for 'Tracy' to be re-interviewed and all the inconsistencies put to her. This was done and she immediately withdrew her allegations.

The reasons why 'Tracy' made these false allegations were never really established. She seemed to enjoy being the centre of attention and was probably not mature enough to appreciate the possible consequences of her actions. But within days of reporting the attack, she was already having second thoughts and had tried to bring the investigation to an end. But by then, she had told so many lies that it was probably difficult for her to completely retract her allegation; that was until she was presented with the Review Team's findings.

'Tracy' was warned about her future conduct. She was lucky. Had she made her allegations a year or so later, she may well have been prosecuted.

CHAPTER 10
'COLD CASE' RAPISTS – FINALLY CONVICTED

It was just before midnight on Saturday 2nd July 1994, when 'Lorraine' (not her real name) was violently attacked by a stranger. 'Lorraine' was then a thirty four year-old single woman, making her way home after a night out with friends. Her route would take her away from the Colchester town centre, up East Hill and into East Street.

As she walked along the street, 'Lorraine' was approached by a man she did not recognise. He politely asked her for directions and she tried to help him, even offering to show him the way. Then, as 'Lorraine' walked off, the man followed her; but as they walked past an off-licence he suddenly dragged her into the car park. There he punched her in the face and threatened to kill her if she screamed. He then forced her to perform oral sex on him.

The attacker then struck 'Lorraine' several times around the head before dragging her further into the car park where he committed a serious sexual assault upon her. Throughout the attack he was threatening to kill her if she made any noise and at one stage he grabbed her by the throat, insisting that she kiss him. When he had finished, the attacker said 'You've got five minutes.'

'Lorraine' was petrified; she thought he meant five minutes to live, but he quickly zipped up his trousers and walked off. For a few minutes, 'Lorraine' lay on the ground not daring to move. Once she was sure he had gone, she staggered to a nearby telephone box and called the police who were there within minutes. 'Lorraine' told them what had happened and she was taken for a medical examination during which various intimate samples were obtained. Despite a search of the area and extensive enquiries by detectives, 'Lorraine's attacker was not identified.

In 2008, a 'Cold Case' review of the original rape investigation was carried out by the Review Team. As a result, a DNA profile of the rapist was developed from semen recovered from 'Lorraine's' thigh.

Unfortunately, the attacker was not on the National DNA Database (NDNAD) so could not be identified. However, the attacker's DNA profile was loaded onto the NDNAD and would be routinely compared with all new DNA profiles being loaded onto the database.

The following year, the Forensic Science Service contacted me saying that the DNA profile of 'Lorraine's' attacker had been matched to a thirty nine year-old Colchester man, Peter Hull. He would have been twenty three years-old at the time of the attack.

I researched Hull's background and found that he had been arrested some months earlier following a domestic incident at his home during which he had committed a minor assault on his partner. Whilst in custody, Hull was routinely finger printed, photographed and a DNA sample obtained. Hull later received a Formal Caution for the assault.

The DNA sample had then been profiled and checked against unsolved crime scene profiles on the NDNAD. It matched 'Lorraine's' attacker. In fact the match was so good that scientists calculated that the chances of her attacker's DNA profile matching someone other than Hull were one in a billion.

The re-investigation was allocated to Stanway Major Investigations Team led by Detective Chief Inspector Godfrey O'Toole. They carried out further enquiries before re-establishing contact with 'Lorraine'. She agreed to support the investigation and any resulting prosecution.

In May 2009, Hull was arrested on suspicion of rape. When interviewed by detectives, Hull said that in 1994, he regularly picked up women in the Colchester area and had sex with them in various places, including their homes, public toilets, Castle Park and even in the churchyard at Hythe Hill. He accepted that he must have had sex with 'Lorraine' as his DNA had been found on her. Nevertheless, he insisted that whenever he had had sex it was always with consent.

On the 21st May 2009, Hull was charged with rape and other sexual offences and was remanded in custody by local magistrates.

In December 2010, Hull, now forty years of age, appeared at Ipswich Crown Court before His Honour Judge John Devaux. He was charged with assault, attempted buggery, attempted rape and rape. He pleaded 'Not Guilty' to all charges.

The prosecution was led by Steven Harvey QC and Hull was represented by Martin Hicks QC, both very successful barristers. 'Lorraine', the main prosecution witness, bravely gave her evidence in court, effectively re-living the terrible events of that summer's night in 1994.

Hull also gave evidence, telling the court that he did not dispute the DNA evidence. However, he claimed that he had never had sex without consent. He went on to say that between 1992 and 1995, he had a number of 'one night stands' in the Colchester area, but could not remember this particular encounter. But he also said that the East Street car park where the attack had occurred, was not a location he would have chosen for sex.

After a six day trial, the jury found him guilty of all charges, except attempted buggery. Mr Hicks then faced the difficult task of mitigation. He told the court that, apart from the common assault on his partner the previous year, Hull had not committed any other offences and did not pose a risk to the public. Hull, he said, had been in a steady relationship for eight years and had two children. He went on to describe the rape as 'out of character ... (committed in) a moment of mental aberration.'

In my view, an expression of regret by Hull himself, would not have gone amiss, especially since his not guilty plea had meant that 'Lorraine' had to give evidence in open court and in the presence of her attacker.

His Honour Judge Devaux said that it was ironic that Hull's assault upon his partner, for which he had received a Caution, had resulted in him being identified as 'Lorraine's' attacker. He told Hull that a lengthy prison term was appropriate. Hull was sentenced to six years imprisonment, less the time he had already spent on remand awaiting trial. He was also placed on the Sex Offender's Register.

Speaking after the trial, DCI O'Toole praised the victim's courage in facing her attacker in court and giving evidence against him; '... a very difficult experience for her.' He went on to say that 'Peter Hull has been sentenced to a significant term of imprisonment and will have time to reflect upon the pain and distress he has caused her.'

This case clearly showed that DNA is one of the most significant developments in the field of criminal investigation; but developing an offender's DNA profile is sometimes of limited assistance. Of course, if the profile matches an individual already on the NDNAD or matches a voluntary DNA sample provided by someone already suspected of that crime, then this will often amount to very strong evidence against him or her.

But what if the offender's DNA profile does not match anyone on the NDNAD; and what if investigators have no idea who committed the crime, then how might the case be resolved? The answer may be for investigators to try a method of investigation historically known as Familial DNA Searching. This approach is based on the fact that half of any individual's DNA is inherited from their mother and the other half from their father. This means that the DNA profiles of close blood relatives, for example, brothers and sisters, though different from each other (except in the case of identical twins) will share more similarities than, say, the DNA profiles of a random group of unrelated individuals will share.

Consequently, where an offender's DNA profile has been found at a crime scene, but he or she is not on the NDNAD, the database can be searched for DNA profiles of individuals that are so similar to the suspect's profile that they could possibly be related to the offender. Then, having produced a list of individuals who could be related to the offender, further work can be carried out to rank them in terms of the likelihood of their actually being related to the offender. Those most likely to be related will appear at the top of the list; and those least likely to be related are at the bottom.

Having received the results of Familial DNA Searching, detectives have then to work their way down the list. They will usually visit each individual on the list, starting at the top, and will interview each one to obtain details of close blood relatives.

If any of those close relatives are already on the NDNAD, they will not be troubled since, if they were the offender, they would already have been identified as the source of the suspect's DNA profile. The relatives who are not already on the NDNAD will then be visited and asked to provide a voluntary DNA sample which will then be profiled and checked against the suspect's DNA profile. Perhaps surprisingly, few people refuse to provide voluntary DNA samples even though they may seal their fate. But if one did refuse, that might only make detectives even more suspicious.

In the past some offenders have tried to escape justice by persuading someone else, perhaps a close friend, to take their place when providing a voluntary DNA sample. Detectives are therefore careful to ensure that the person who provides the voluntary DNA sample is who they purport to be.

The Familial DNA Searching method was first successfully used in the United Kingdom in 2003 by Operation Glitter detectives investigating the death of fifty three year-old lorry driver Michael 'Micky' Little. Michael, who worked for the Ford Motor Company, was killed around 12.30am on the 21st March 2003, after a brick thrown from a footbridge over the M3 in Surrey, went through the windscreen of the lorry he was driving. The brick struck him on the chest, but miraculously, he managed to drive the lorry onto to the hard shoulder before dying of heart failure.

Surrey Police launched a murder investigation. They were sure that that the killer lived locally because the footbridge from which the brick had been thrown was a shortcut between Camberley and Frimley. It was frequently used by local people after a night out.

Enquiries revealed that shortly before that incident, there had been an unsuccessful attempt to steal a Renault Clio parked in a driveway in Brackendale Road, Camberley. The would-be thieves had smashed the car window and then tried to hotwire the car before making off towards the motorway footbridge. One of the suspects left blood in the Clio. They also took two house bricks from a driveway further along the road.

A DNA profile was developed from blood recovered from the Clio and that profile matched the DNA profile found on the brick police had recovered from the lorry's cab. An ethnic marker within the DNA profile also indicated that the suspect was a white male. The DNA profile was searched on the National DNA Database (NDNAD), but the offender was not on it. Three hundred and fifty local people gave voluntary DNA samples, but still the offender was not identified. Detectives decided to try a new procedure then known as Familial DNA Searching.

The NDNAD was searched for people having a similar DNA profile to the suspect's profile, but only the profiles of white males living in Surrey or Hampshire were checked. As a result, twenty five people were identified. The one with the most similar DNA profile had the surname Harman.

Voluntary DNA samples were taken from Harman's relatives, one of whom was Craig Harman, a nineteen year-old shop assistant who lived in Frimley. The DNA profile developed from his DNA sample matched the killer's DNA profile.

Harman was arrested on 30th October 2003. He was subsequently charged with murder, attempting to steal a car and the theft of two house bricks.

On the 19th April 2004, at the Old Bailey, Harman (now twenty years-old) pleaded guilty to manslaughter. He admitted having thrown the brick to '... annoy drivers and interfere with traffic flow.' He was sentenced to six years imprisonment.

Essex Police 'Cold Case' officers first used this method in 2009, following a review of a 'Stranger Rape' investigation codenamed Operation Pilgrim.

On the evening of Thursday 11th December 1997, a fifteen year-old Harlow schoolgirl, 'Jenny' (not her real name) attended a concert at Mark Hall School, where she was regarded as a promising pupil. 'Jenny' was a saxophonist and intended staying for the whole concert even though she was not actually performing during the second half. However, during the interval she learnt that her boyfriend had gone home as he had felt unwell.

'Jenny' sought permission to leave the concert early and was soon walking along a route that would take her through the underpass at the A414, which then took her into Momples Road. There was plenty of traffic in the area, but no other pedestrians.

By 8.50pm, 'Jenny' was crossing an unlit grassed hillock that would eventually bring her to Churchfield. As she walked down the other side of the hillock into an area known locally as Ten Metre Wood, 'Jenny' heard someone behind her. She thought it was probably a jogger and stepped to one side.

Suddenly she was hit from behind and on turning round saw a man in a stocking mask, directly behind her. He struck her on the face saying, 'If you scream again I am going to kill you and I am going to kill you bad.'

He ordered her to take her school uniform off and fearing what he might do, 'Jenny' said. 'If I let you do what you do will you not hurt me and let me go?' He replied, 'Yeah.'

'Jenny' took her trousers off and the man indecently assaulted, then raped her, telling her to enjoy it. At one stage, 'Jenny' told her attacker that she was HIV positive. She was not, but she hoped this might put him off; however, he just replied, 'So am I.'

The man then stopped, adjusted his clothing and ran off towards First Avenue.

'Jenny' went to her boyfriend's house and her mother was called. She took both of them to Harlow Police Station where the attack was reported.

A major investigation was launched led by Detective Superintendent (later Chief Superintendent) Brian Storey. 'Jenny' was medically examined and various forensic samples taken from her. A DNA profile of the attacker was later developed from those samples, but subsequent checks of the National DNA Database (NDNAD) failed to identify him.

The area where the attack took place was searched, but no forensic or other evidence was recovered.

The attack was well publicised and even featured on 'Crimewatch'. A number of witnesses came forward saying they had seen a man who fitted the description given by 'Jenny', in and around the area at the material time. One produced an e-fit picture of the attacker, copies of which were widely distributed.

Detective Superintendent Storey decided to carry out a mass DNA screening operation targeting local white males of between fifteen and forty years of age. Over one hundred and twenty voluntary DNA samples were obtained, but none matched the rapist.

An offender profiler was consulted to see if a they could 'paint a picture' of the attacker, for example how old he was, where he might live or work, what trouble he may have already been in with the police, etc. But no new suspects were identified and eventually the investigation wound down.

In 2011, a 'Cold Case' review was conducted by the Review Team. It was led by Phil Parker. Nine boxes of case material were recovered from the archives and examined over a period of several weeks. Phil concluded that there was probably only one way to resolve this crime which was via Familial DNA Searching.

The re-investigation was passed to the newly formed Cold Case *Investigation* Team (CCIT) led by Detective Chief Inspector Rob Vinson. They liaised with forensic scientists and they produced a list of suspects who had DNA profiles similar to the man who had attacked 'Jenny'. Those suspects would be visited to obtain full details of close relatives. The team also traced 'Jenny' who was now married and living in London. She readily agreed to support a re-investigation of this attack.

One of the first men visited by detectives was Frank Molt. He had provided a DNA sample in December 2009, following his arrest on suspicion of causing death by careless driving. The casualty, a seventy one year-old pedestrian, was struck as he crossed Epping High Street and subsequently died. Detectives established that Frank Molt had two sons. Both were visited so that voluntary DNA samples could be obtained from them. The DNA profile of one, thirty four year-old airport worker Jon Molt, matched the rapist's DNA profile and enquiries revealed that he was living in Harlow at the time of the attack.

In January 2012, Jon Molt, now married with two children, was arrested and interviewed about the attack. He gave a statement to detectives in which he denied raping the girl. Nevertheless he was charged with the attack on 'Jenny' and remanded in custody to await trial.

In June 2012, Jon Molt appeared at Chelmsford Crown Court before His Honour Judge Christopher Ball QC. He pleaded not guilty to rape. Prosecution Counsel Carolyn Gardiner told the court that the probability of the semen recovered from 'Jenny' not coming from Jon Molt was one in a billion. 'Members of the jury,' she said, 'just think what a huge number that is.'

I was not in court, but Molt's evidence, which was widely reported, was somewhat mystifying. In particular, Molt allegedly said that he had a problem with his memory which was getting progressively worse. However, he produced no medical evidence supporting this claim.

Molt accepted that it was his DNA that had been recovered from swabs taken from 'Jenny' during her medical examination. He also accepted the victim's account of what had happened to her, but said he could not remember the incident.

During cross examination he said, 'I cannot remember putting a stocking mask over my head. I cannot deny or confirm it. I cannot remember seeing her walking across the field in her school uniform ... I've no recollection I grabbed her, threatened her or held her down.'

Could *anyone* who had once committed such a crime ever forget it?

He was asked about any other rapes he may have committed around that time. He said, 'I can't tell you. As far as I can tell you I think not.'

Finally, Molt said that if he had been able to remember anything, he would have admitted it. 'I wouldn't want to put anyone through this sort of process.'

But he did.

On the 11th June 2012, the jury of six men and six women found Jon Molt guilty of rape. Their verdict was unanimous. His wife broke down in tears and had to be ushered from the court screaming, 'He didn't do it.'

Sentencing Molt to eight and a half years imprisonment, Judge Ball slated Molt for not pleading guilty at an earlier hearing, thus forcing his victim to re-live it all. He said, 'By pleading not guilty it meant that the victim was forced to drag from the depths of her memory that which she had hoped to put behind her and relive it all. I have looked at the risk you pose and the harm you caused and need to send a message designed to deter others from doing this and to reassure the public.' He ordered that Molt should serve two thirds of his sentence before he could apply for parole and placed him on the Sex Offender's Register for life.

After the trial, 'Jenny' told reporters that she felt a sense of relief now that her attacker had been caught. She thanked Essex Police and the forensic scientists for their work and said she strongly supported the maintenance of the National DNA Database.

'Jenny' was later interviewed on the Dave Monk Show on BBC Essex Radio. She spoke about how she had 'survived' the attack. 'Jenny' said that when she first went back into her classroom after the attack, the class fell silent and looked at her. Then, a girl she hardly knew started talking to her and everyone relaxed after that. She spoke about the fact that she had no control over what had happened to her, but that she did have the choice not to let it affect her. 'Jenny' said that she continued to work hard at school, got married and was now enjoying a successful career as a scientist. Finally, she urged other victims who had endured similar experiences to tell the police who, '... will believe you and support you every step of the way.'

Also commenting after the trial, the Senior Investigating Officer said, 'Jon Molt believed for over fourteen years that he had got away with this brutal and shocking attack on a young girl who had just left a school carol concert ... This prosecution sends a clear message to those who commit such crimes that they should spend their days expecting a knock on the door, no matter how long ago their offence.'

This was not an idle comment. Essex Police, like most other forces, now has the DNA profiles of a number of offenders who are presently unknown; but they won't always remain so.

CHAPTER 11
THE DEATH OF MAURICE SAMS

One of the more unusual 'Cold Case' reviews conducted by the Review Team concerned the alleged suicide of Maurice Sams. He was found dead inside his caravan at Tollesbury, near Chelmsford, on the 23rd July 1951. The blackened end of a hosepipe was found on the ground below the exhaust pipe of his Austin car. Clearly it had once been connected to the exhaust pipe itself. The other end of the hosepipe had been fed through one of the caravan's windows resulting in Maurice's death from carbon monoxide poisoning. The car engine was no longer running, it having run out of petrol.

Maurice had never threatened to take his own life and no suicide note was found. Nonetheless, an Inquest into his death, held the following week, recorded a verdict of 'Suicide' and his body was cremated. But had he deliberately taken his own life or could this death have been accidental; perhaps even murder?

The review began in 2004 after Maurice's son, Nigel, learnt of the recent formation of the Major Crime Review Team. Nigel explained that he was only about three years-old when his father had died and his mother had since re-married. Some years ago, Nigel's step-father died and Nigel asked his mother for some personal items to remember him by. In due course she sent him various documents and it was information contained within those documents that caused Maurice to suspect that his father's death may not have been suicide after all.

Nigel initially contacted Chelmsford CID, however, they were unable to assist him. He then contacted the Essex Coroner who sent him a copy of the Inquest file, which he then studied. Convinced that all was not as it had once seemed, Nigel contacted the Review Team outlining his concerns.

Nigel accepted that in all probability, if his father's death had been accidental, little could now be done to put the record straight. Worse still, if it had been murder made to look like suicide, it would be virtually impossible to prosecute his killer(s) as they are probably now infirm or dead. Furthermore, over fifty years had since elapsed so any witness evidence that might still be available would now be considered too unreliable.

So was there any real point in re-examining the facts of this case? Nigel believed there was. In 1951 suicide was still a criminal offence and in some eyes there was (and perhaps still is) a certain stigma attached to it. Nigel hoped that if a 'Cold Case' review of his father's death found that the 'Suicide' verdict was unsafe, an 'Open' verdict might be substituted and his late father's name and reputation restored.

Whether or not a 'Cold Case' review of Maurice's death was a good use of police resources was debatable. But even if it only resulted in the original 'Suicide' verdict being reconsidered and an 'Open' verdict substituted, it would still bring the family some peace of mind.

In due course Nigel forwarded various document to me, including personal papers, extracts of the Coroner's file and copies of newspaper reports of the time. From these it was possible to examine the sequence of events leading up to, and following, Maurice Sams' death.

However, this review revealed a web of intrigue that would not have looked out of place in an Agatha Christie novel!

Maurice Sams was thirty seven years-old when he died. He was a partner in a garage-cum-taxi business B C Cannon and Company of Puckeridge, Hertfordshire. The firm had experienced some financial problems, mainly due to the inclement weather that had affected the coach hire part of his business. But documents later revealed that Maurice's partner had injected some capital into the company and both men were more optimistic about the future of the business.

Maurice was married to Marguerite and the couple lived in St Michael's Road, Broxbourne, with their daughter Yvonne and son, Nigel. A second daughter, Cheryl was born after Maurice's death. Like most couples, the Sams had their 'ups and downs'. Mrs Sams was especially concerned about Maurice's membership of Bonningtons Country Club at Hunsdon, Hertfordshire, where he seemed to be spending more and more time. She also suspected that he may have become just a little too friendly with a woman who worked there, behind the bar.

In fact, Mrs Sams was so concerned that she shared her suspicions with her solicitor and acting on her instructions, he hired a firm of private detectives to find out what, if anything, her husband was up to.

On Tuesday 17th July 1951, two private detectives went to the club. They described it as a seven bedroomed private club of some seventy five acres, catering for those with an interest in horse riding and fishing. At that time it was owned and run by Clifford and Ruth Berkelmans.

The private detectives obtained temporary membership and after tea, spent the evening in the bar engaging Ruth in polite conversation. During their discussions, Ruth told them that her husband Clifford had just sold a yacht for £3,000. She also mentioned that her daughter 'Ella' (not her real name) was coming home from boarding school on Friday, and showed them photographs of her.

During the subsequent enquiry into Maurice Sams' death, Clifford Berkelmans told police that around 11pm the following day (Wednesday 18th) Maurice told him he was going to drive to his boat which was moored off the Essex coast.

Clifford said he had suggested to Maurice that he should instead go home and said he would follow him. Maurice, however, did not want to be followed, took the ignition key out of Clifford's car and refused to hand it over. A fight ensued, but according to Clifford, '...no serious hurt was caused.'

Clifford said that the following day (Thursday 19th) he had driven to Tollesbury to help Maurice with his caravan. Unfortunately, as neither had brought any wheels with them they could not move it, so both returned to the club. Maurice allegedly apologised for his behaviour the previous night.

The next day (Friday 20th) Maurice drove to St Osyth, near the Essex seaside town of Clacton, to pick up his wife. She later told police that when she saw her husband he had some facial injuries, including a black eye, scratches on his nose and a swollen right cheek. His right wrist was also bandaged.

Maurice told her he had been involved in an accident, but he did not elaborate.

Later that day, one of the private detectives returned to the club to continue his observations; but Maurice did not appear. During the evening the detective saw the Berkelmans' teenage daughter 'Ella' eating with an older woman. He recognised her from the photographs previously shown to him by Ruth Berkelmans. He assumed the older woman was the girl's grandmother.

The following morning (Saturday 21st) Maurice returned home where he had breakfast with his wife. He did not tell her where he had stayed the previous night. Around 11am, he left home to visit his father who later told police that Maurice appeared to be in good health. Later that day the private detective returned to the club and was there when Maurice returned. He kept observations on Maurice and during the evening saw him leaving the bar, followed shortly by Ruth.

The detective waited a while, but the couple did not return so he began looking around. He ended up in the grounds where he saw Maurice walking back towards the club from the direction of the club's fishing lake. Maurice was being supported by Ruth and her daughter 'Ella'. The detective noticed that Maurice's hands were bandaged and that his clothes were now dirty and torn. The clothing appeared to be clinging to Maurice's body as thought he had actually been in the lake. The two women walked Maurice to the rear of the club and he was not seen alive after that.

Around 11pm, a worried looking Ruth returned to the bar and called time.

The following day (Sunday 22nd) the private detective returned to the club where he resumed his observations. He did not see either Maurice or Ruth at the club; and Clifford did not make an appearance until 9pm.

The next morning, (Monday 23rd) Maurice was found dead; he was lying on a bunk bed in his caravan. A three quarters full bottle of whisky was lying on the floor. The local police officer, Constable Duncombe, had been making enquiries into a Buick motor car found abandoned in a nearby ditch when he discovered what appeared to him to be a case of suicide.

The officer did not find a suicide or other note, but on searching the body he did find documents relating to unpaid bills, a surrendered life insurance policy and a pawn ticket for a watch.

Maurice's body was removed to Colchester Hospital where a post mortem examination was carried out the following day. Amongst other things, the pathologist noted two black eyes and blood inside the deceased's nostrils. The cause of death was given as carbon monoxide poisoning. Perhaps surprisingly, the Inquest at Witham Coroner's Court was held later the same week, on Friday 27th July 1951. After considering the evidence before him, the Coroner recorded a verdict of 'Suicide' and Maurice was cremated three days later on Monday 30th July 1951. This was just one week after his death.

Witness statements and newspaper reports of the time summarised the main evidence given at the Inquest. Clifford Berkelmans' evidence was that Maurice had been coming to the club for about six months. Maurice, he said, was morose and unhappy at home; he was also in financial difficulties. Berkelmans recounted their fight the previous Wednesday and spoke about Maurice's movements the day before his death. Maurice, he said, had left the club in his car around 12.30pm, en-route to his caravan. He and his wife followed an hour or so later, but arrived at the caravan before Maurice. He then joined them saying that he had crashed his car into a ditch whilst avoiding two children.

Berkelmans said that the three of them went back to the club where Maurice remained until 5pm. When Maurice finally left he told them he was going to his garage to get a breakdown vehicle so as to recover his car. Later that evening, he allegedly telephoned Clifford Berkelmans, either drunk or excited, but the line went dead. Berkelmans said he got the impression that Maurice was greatly depressed at having put his car in the ditch.

Clifford Berkelmans told the Coroner that Maurice had said that his life '...wasn't worth living'; also that he had, '...nothing to live for'. However, Berkelmans also said that although unhappy, Maurice had never spoken about taking his own life. Nevertheless, his evidence may have significantly influenced the Coroner who was trying to determine Maurice's state of mind around the time of his death.

In short, Berkelmans had described Maurice as morose, unhappy at home, in financial difficulties and greatly depressed about the car crash. But how reliable was his evidence? True, Maurice was having problems at home, but no one was suggesting that things were *so* serious that he was either considering or being threatened with divorce. His business had gone through a rough time, but things were improving. Mention was also made of bills totaling £1250 and the fact that his business account was overdrawn. But the Letters of Administration later showed that the net value of his estate far exceeded his debts.

A £3,000 cheque stub made out to the club, was also found in his cheque book. This was the same sum that Ruth had mentioned to the private detectives when she told them about the recent sale of her husband's yacht. If the cheque stub related to the purchase of Clifford Berkelmans' yacht and Berkelmans genuinely thought Maurice was in financial difficulties, why had he accepted a £3,000 cheque from him? Furthermore, why had Maurice bought this yacht at all if he was in financial difficulties?

There were also discrepancies with Clifford Berkelmans' account of their movements the previous Sunday. Berkelmans was unaware of the fact that Maurice had been the subject of a surveillance operation for most of that week, including that particular Sunday.

The private detective who was specifically at the club to observe Maurice, did not see him around 12.30pm that Sunday when Maurice had allegedly left the club; nor did he see the Berkelmans leave an hour or so later. He also failed to spot the three returning later that afternoon; and did not see Maurice leaving again around 5pm.

In short, the detective saw nothing at all of either Maurice or Ruth that day; and he did not see Clifford before 9pm that evening.

The fishing lake incident also remained unexplained and with the Berkelmans now dead it would be necessary to trace and to interview their daughter 'Ella'.

In due course 'Ella' was traced to another part of the country, but she was unwilling to be interviewed. Fortunately, I found out that she was due to visit a family friend who lived near her former home and so made an unannounced visit to this friend, 'accidentally' bumping into 'Ella' at the same time.

'Ella' was not particularly helpful, saying that she could remember nothing of the reported events. 'Ella' confirmed that her grandmother had indeed lived with the family, but she denied being the girl allegedly seen having dinner with her that Friday evening in July 1951. However, she could not suggest who the girl might have been. 'Ella' also said that a number of women worked behind the bar and if one was having an affair with Maurice (who she did not know by name) it was not necessarily her mother. In particular, she denied having helped her mother assist anyone from the fishing lake.

But what motive would the private detective have had for making up such a story? And if it had happened as he described, is it likely that 'Ella' could have forgotten helping her mother support an injured and soaking wet man coming from the direction of the fishing lake?

Looking back, it appears that a number of the individuals directly or indirectly involved in these events, failed to tell either the police or the Coroner what they knew. Firstly, Mrs Sams did not tell either the police or the Coroner that her husband had been under surveillance during the days leading up to his death. Had she done so, the private detectives may have been called to give evidence, thus revealing some inconsistencies in the accounts given by others, especially Clifford Berkelmans.

Secondly, Mrs Berkelmans failed to tell the police about the incident near the lake, which could have resulted from an assault or have been a failed suicide attempt. This information would have been important to a Coroner considering whether Maurice had had an accident, been assaulted or taken his own life.

Next, the private detective who witnessed the incident near the lake and days later, had learnt of Maurice's 'suicide', must also have wondered whether or not the lake incident may have been an assault or failed suicide attempt.

If so, it was something that could be relevant to the police enquiry and the subsequent Inquest. However, he did not inform either the police or the Coroner. Instead, he submitted a written report to the solicitor who had instructed him, a copy of which was forwarded to Mrs Sams some ten days later. She also failed to share the report with the police, as did her solicitor.

Interestingly, records showed that the private detectives' bill came to £34.15s 6d (about £34.75p). It included temporary membership of the club, their surveillance work, drinks, meals and the cost of their hire car, which had also ended up in a ditch! Quite good value for money!

Having read all the papers, I then submitted the original post mortem report to a Home Office Pathologist for his views, mainly because the blood found in Maurice's nose had not been satisfactorily explained. He subsequently reported that such bleeding was not uncommon in cases of carbon monoxide poisoning and that it did not necessarily indicate that Maurice had been assaulted. Overall, he agreed with the original cause of death and said that none of the injuries found during the post mortem examination had contributed to Maurice's death.

Having completed the review, my overall conclusions were that there was no medical or other evidence to show that Maurice had been murdered. However, the possibility that a third party introduced the hosepipe into the caravan as Maurice lay sleeping, could not be entirely discounted.

But if this was a straightforward case of suicide, why had questionable, sometimes contradictory evidence, been given to the police and to the Coroner; and why had there been so much secrecy?

It also seemed strange that Maurice should commit suicide in his caravan. If he intended dying, it would have been far easier and more effective had he put the hosepipe into the car and locked himself inside. The car's interior is much smaller than that of a caravan and would have quickly filled with exhaust fumes, thus hastening his death.

Perhaps it was a 'cry for help' and Maurice never really intended to kill himself. Maybe he mistakenly believed that the caravan was too large a space for the carbon monoxide fumes to fill it. Perhaps he thought that Clifford Berkelmans would respond to his abandoned telephone call that Sunday night and 'discover' him trying to kill himself?

Unfortunately, the main parties involved in these events have long since died and no fresh lines of enquiry had emerged. But what if anything might now be done about the original suicide verdict?

The current law in relation to suicide is quite specific, although this may not have been the case in 1951. 'Suicide' is defined as, 'Voluntarily doing an act for the purpose of destroying one's own life while one is conscious of what one is doing.'

Inquest verdicts are decided on the civil standard of proof known as the balance of probabilities i.e. *is it more likely than not* that such and such happened. But in reality, a Coroner considering a verdict of 'Suicide' requires far more than that. S/he will look for evidence of a conscious intention by the deceased, to take his or her own life, for example a suicide note, verbal statements, etc.

What evidence was there that Maurice Sams had intended to take his life? The answer is not perhaps as much as the Coroner may have been led to believe.

Maurice left no suicide note and no evidence was given to show that he had ever threatened or attempted to commit suicide before. And even if the incident at the country club lake had been a failed suicide attempt, the Coroner was unaware of it so would not have taken it into account when deciding his verdict.

Furthermore, apart from Clifford Berkelmans' evidence, there was nothing else to suggest that Maurice's matrimonial or financial positions were *so* bad that he would even have contemplated suicide. Could they have been as bad as had been portrayed if he had just purchased a £3,000 yacht?

So how could the Coroner have been so sure that Maurice had intended to commit suicide?

Perhaps an 'Open' verdict might have been more appropriate since the Coroner had no direct evidence to show that Maurice had intended to commit suicide and so could not entirely rule out other possibilities e.g. accident or even homicide.

Nigel Sams hoped that in the light of all the information now available, the Essex Coroner might be willing and able to quash the original 'Suicide' verdict and substitute it with an 'Open' verdict'.

Unfortunately, Coroners can only exercise their powers to enquire into a death once and in this case, had already done so.

Nigel's only option was to apply to the High Court, via the Attorney General, to have the original verdict quashed on humanitarian grounds and a new Inquest convened. This can be done even if the fresh Inquest is likely to come to the same conclusion as the first. But there needs to be new evidence which was not available to the original Inquest, evidence which *may* have made a material difference.

In this case (largely through Nigel's Sams' efforts) evidence has been discovered that had been withheld from the Coroner; and that evidence *may* have made a difference.

Firstly, both the police and the Coroner were unaware of the fact that Maurice had been under surveillance during the week before his death. They were, therefore, unaware of the fishing lake incident and the fact that the private detectives' evidence contradicted parts of Clifford Berkelmans' accounts, thus creating question marks over his reliability.

Secondly, Berkelmans was the main witness in respect of Maurice's possibly 'suicidal' state of mind. He described Maurice as morose, unhappy at home, in financial difficulties and greatly depressed about the car crash. Yet it appears that Clifford may have accepted a £3,000 cheque from him?

It was also later established that Maurice's assets more than covered his liabilities, but this was not known until months after the Inquest.

Nigel had now to decide whether or not to start the appeal process and was notified accordingly. Still determined to resolve the mystery, Nigel wrote to the Attorney General asking that the original 'Suicide' verdict be set aside.

In due course he received an application form for a High Court hearing, but after carefully considering the huge cost of making an application to the High Court and the emotional strain this was putting him and his family under, he reluctantly decided not to proceed.

Nigel remains convinced that his father death may have been accidental, or that he was murdered and his death made to look like suicide.

In my view, it seems more likely than not that Maurice took his own life. However, I believe that the evidence supporting this is not sufficiently conclusive and that if an Inquest into his death was to be held today and *all* the facts considered, it would possibly result in an 'Open' verdict'. This is because there is, in my opinion, little evidence to show to the evidential standard required, that Sams really intended to take his own life.

Finally, reading newspaper reports of this case was interesting as they 'shone a light' on life in the early 1950's. Apart from reports on the case, the newspapers also contained other interesting news items of the day, including a report on the sale at Christies, of Constable's painting 'Stratford Mill on the Stour'. It went for a mere £44,100.

Another news item reported that a sentence of seven years preventive detention, imposed at Essex Quarter Sessions on one George William Priddy, of no fixed abode, was reduced to twelve month imprisonment by the Court of Appeal.

Delivering the court's judgement the Lord Chief Justice, Lord Goddard, said that a seven year sentence for stealing a pint of milk '... seemed to sound wrong.'

He was obviously a master of the understatement!

CHAPTER 12
ABDUCTION BY GYPSIES?

Sometimes the Review Team is allocated a review simply because the enquiry does not seem to be any other team's responsibility! Perhaps the most unusual review we were ever asked to conduct, concerned the alleged abduction of a baby, decades ago, by a gypsy family.

When I first heard the allegations they reminded me of the fear of gypsies that used to exist in the area of east London I grew up in. My mother, for example, would not answer the front door to gypsy women selling 'lucky heather' for fear that if she refused to buy some, they would put a curse on her.

Also, as children, we used to recite a rhyme that went something like this:

'My mother said, I never should, play with the gypsies in the wood. If I did, she would say, naughty boy to disobey.'

The message seemed to be that if we went into the woods and played with the gypsies, we might come to some harm. I have not established the origins of that rhyme, but I imagine it was something that parents told their children to stop them wandering off and talking to strangers. In fact, it is said that the story of 'Little Red Riding Hood' had the same objective.

Our review of this alleged abduction began after a retired police officer gave a talk about historical crimes in Essex. As a result, a member of the audience later contacted the speaker enquiring about a possible unsolved 'Cold Case', the abduction of a child who allegedly went missing sometime between 1928 and 1933. In order to protect the identities of all parties I have given them pseudonyms.

Briefly, the audience member, 'Mr Roberts', said that his eighty three year-old mother, 'Alice Roberts', had recently told him that she had been kidnapped as a child and brought up in Eastwood (just outside Southend-on-Sea) by a gypsy couple, 'Tom and Jane Adams'. One day 'Jane' allegedly told 'Alice' that in 1929 she had given birth to a baby.

The birth had been registered, but whilst breast feeding, 'Jane' had fallen asleep and had unfortunately smothered the baby. The authorities were not informed and the baby was secretly buried. 'Jane' had gone on to say that 'Alice' had been kidnapped to take the dead baby's place.

All that was known about 'Alice's' natural parents was that they were religious and came from Rochford, Essex.

The ex-police officer, who had given the talk, began to have concerns about the allegations and the information was eventually passed to the Review Team.

Over the years there have been many stories and 'urban myths' about gypsies kidnapping babies and children; and these continue today. It would therefore have been easy to dismiss this particular story; but it was not simply the story of an unknown person allegedly abducted by gypsies. We had her name and it would not be too difficult to look into her family background.

We decided that some further enquiries should be made since, if what 'Alice' had told her son was true, there was a dead baby who had been secretly buried somewhere, a family whose baby had been stolen and 'Alice', the adult survivor of that abduction.

There were two families to identify. One was 'Alice's' natural family and the other, the family of the alleged 'kidnappers'. I arranged to meet 'Mr Roberts' in person to find out what I could. He came across as a normal, level headed individual, who appeared simply to be trying to deal with his mother's allegations, which had come completely 'out of the blue'. He had already carried out some local research in an attempt to prove or disprove what his mother had alleged. So far he had been unsuccessful.

'Mr Roberts' said it had all begun when he told his mother he was thinking about compiling his family tree. 'Alice' was growing older and her physical health declining, so she decided to tell him about her 'mother's' revelations. 'Alice' told him that she would love to meet any surviving members of her 'real' family, but if none were still alive, she wished to be buried with them and to have her 'real' name on her gravestone.

I asked 'Mr Roberts' about his mother and about anything else she had told him concerning her earlier life. He said that she had told him she had no photographs of herself prior to the age of eight. She had also spoken of being psychologically tortured to make her forget her real name, including threats to set her on fire and to kill her. 'Alice' also told him that there were times when, as a child, she was not fed, was locked in a cupboard and was treated totally differently to her siblings. She never went to school and was excluded from various aspects of family life.

'Alice' said she got married when aged twenty one and remained with her husband until his death in 1997.

In essence, 'Alice' told her son that she had lived almost her entire life using the identity of the dead child she had allegedly replaced.

I asked 'Mr Roberts' if he knew who exactly had been involved in the alleged abduction. He said that as far as he knew, it was only 'Jane Adams'. However, she and a few close members of the family allegedly knew about it, but they were all now dead. He also said that all of his mother's siblings were born after the alleged abduction so probably knew nothing about it; but they obviously knew that *something* had happened because of the different way their mother treated 'Alice'. Furthermore, 'Jane' and 'Albert' would allegedly talk about 'Alice' saying, 'She is not of our blood.'

'Mr Robert's' said that much of the information about 'Alice's' background had actually come from one of her aunts who had since died. The aunt had allegedly told 'Alice' that her real parents came from '... more than a good home and family.' He was able to provide me with a family tree; but had no information about the child who was allegedly smothered, or about the alleged abduction itself.

In due course we commenced a review. I first contacted a local historian (and ex-police sergeant) Leonard Sellers who had just published a book entitled, 'Eastwood, Essex: A History'. I knew that it had taken him many years to research it and felt sure he would be aware of any significant historical crimes, such as the abduction of a baby.

I spoke to Len and he told me he had not heard of any such abduction; however, the book confirmed that there was a gypsy community living in Eastwood at the relevant time.

I concluded that without some further investigation, it would not be possible to prove or disprove the information provided by 'Mr Roberts'. I recommended that 'Alice' should be formally interviewed as a vulnerable victim. That way we could obtain and preserve her evidence and do so in a sensitive way. At the same time, 'Alice' could be asked to provide a voluntary DNA sample from which her DNA profile could be developed.

I also recommended that enquiries be made in relation to 'Jane Adams' and her children ('Alice's' alleged siblings). If we already had, or could develop, DNA profiles of them, it should be possible to confirm or otherwise, that 'Alice' was biologically related to them.

The investigation was allocated to Brentwood Major Investigations Team. In due course, 'Alice' was interviewed and a voluntary DNA sample obtained from her. This was compared with the DNA profiles of members of 'Jane Adams' family; and it matched. 'Alice' had not, therefore, been born into a different family, which meant that she had not after all, been abducted to replace a dead child.

Both 'Alice' and her son were informed accordingly.

How or why she came to believe what she did is a mystery. I am sure she was not acting maliciously and that in her case the mind really was playing tricks. But what she had told her son could have been true so it needed to be resolved.

At least, by investigating what she had said, we have finally laid her concerns to rest.

CHAPTER 13
FATAL INDUSTRIAL ACCIDENTS

The investigation of Fatal Industrial Accidents (also known as Work Related Deaths) was once the sole responsibility of the Health and Safety Executive (HSE).

Years ago, when attending workplace deaths, police officers used almost to breathe a sigh of relief when told that HSE Inspectors were on their way! They were the experts in health and safety legislation, safe systems of work, etc., and had all this knowledge and the necessary technical expertise to call upon in order to deal with these sometimes very complicated matters.

However, there came a time when society began to challenge the notion that 'accidents just happen'; also, that if death or serious injury occurred in the workplace, it was appropriate to deal with these incidents simply as breaches of health and safety legislation.

Obviously there are situations when accidents do 'just happen'; for example, during a freak storm lightning strikes a telegraph pole which falls onto an engineer sheltering nearby in his van. It is difficult to see how any resulting death or serious injury could have been avoided. And sometimes it is the deceased's own reckless or negligent action that caused their own death. For example, contrary to work protocols, the same engineer actually climbs the telegraph pole during a storm and is struck by lightning.

But on some occasions, death occurs as a result of a another individual and / or an organisation's negligence. And if their actions or inactions are really serious, they may amount to the commission of criminal offences such as Gross Negligent or Corporate Manslaughter. That is in addition to any relevant breaches of health and safety legislation.

The first Fatal Industrial Accident I was asked to review followed the death of a welder who was killed whilst working inside a road tanker which had been previously been used to transport petrol.

Apparently the tanker needed a metal patch to be welded to the bulkhead and when the welder was inside the tanker, an explosion ripped through the vehicle, killing him instantly.

When first learning of the incident, my initial reaction was that climbing inside a petrol tanker with a blowtorch was not something I could ever have been persuaded to do. However, I understand that it would be perfectly safe to do this if the tanker had been properly cleaned of flammable / explosive substances and purged of all fumes, before the welding work started.

The main questions to be answered in this particular case were had this been done and if not, who was accountable for any acts or omissions that resulted in this explosion. For example, had the welder's employer negligently failed to prevent the tanker from containing petrol or petrol fumes, failed to provide adequate warnings or failed to provide safe appliances, machinery, plant or works? In other words, had the employer taken all reasonable and necessary precautions to ensure that the welder was not taking avoidable risks when he began working with welding gear in a tanker which had once contained petrol and /or fumes?

The situation was unclear so I recommended that a criminal investigation should be carried out in order to establish the full facts. This was undertaken by the Brentwood Major Investigations Team. In due course, both criminal and civil proceedings were instigated.

In February 2007, at Basildon Crown Court, the manslaughter charge was dismissed by the judge. However, the company was fined £5,000, with £20,000 costs, for beaching the 1974 Health and Safety at Work Act; and the Managing Director was fined £10,000 for breaching Section 37(1) of the same act.

During the years following that review, there have been numerous prosecutions of individuals and organisations in relation to work related deaths. Now, when such incidents occur, a Senior Investigating Officer (SIO) will attend the scene, together with Health and Safety Inspectors. Together they will decide how the matter is to be investigated. At the very least, the SIO will end up preparing a report for H M Coroner.

Generally speaking, a Review Team will not normally conduct reviews of Fatal Industrial Accidents; however, in certain circumstances Chief Officers will still ask them to do so. This could be, for example, where a death occurs locally, but could have nationwide ramifications.

Take, for example, a case where a person employed by a nationwide energy supply company is killed whilst working at a local depot. In theory, other workers employed at similar sites across the UK may have already been killed or injured in similar circumstances; or may still be at risk.

The local SIO will be focused on the death that s/he is investigating, but Chief Officers may require an urgent review to be carried out to see if the investigation should be expanded nationwide.

As part of their review, the Review Team would liaise with the Health and Safety Executive who, apart from having knowledge of any similar incidents, also has the power and infrastructure to impose any necessary and urgent safety protocols on the industry.

CHAPTER 14
MISSING PERSONS FOUND DEAD

If person goes missing and their life is possibly at risk, the family expects a professional response from the police and other emergency services. If the missing person (MISPER) is later found dead, Chief Officers will want to be assured that the force had carried out all reasonable enquiries and in a timely fashion, in order to find the MISPER before s/he died.

Consequently, Chief Officers will enquire into all MISPERS Found Dead, in each case seeking the views of the area's police commander, about the local investigation. Sometimes, concerns emerge which can only be confirmed or allayed by a MISPER Found Dead Review. Some of those initial concerns are quite understandable; but once the full facts have been established, things are not always as concerning as they first appeared.

Occasionally, the Review Team will also be tasked to carry out a review of an ongoing MISPER investigation. This is to see if any opportunities to resolve it have been overlook and to confirm, or otherwise, that the investigation is being adequately resourced and properly managed.

A review will begin with a briefing by the Investigating Officer. As with other types of review, the reviewer will then study all paperwork and computer records generated by the investigation. The task has been made a little easier in Essex because of the introduction of COMPACT (described in chapter 4). This database is where most of the information about the MISPER investigation can be found.

One of the first and most important assessments to be made is whether or not the MISPER'S Risk Level was appropriate. When a person is reported missing, investigators will decide if they are a Low, Medium or High MISPER. A Low Risk MISPER may be an adult who has not arrived at their destination when they were expected to. However, they are normally capable of looking after themselves and there are no real concerns about their health, safety or well-being. However, a High Risk MISPER is a matter of real concern. They may, for example, be a person with mental health problems who has run away to commit suicide. Clearly they need to be found as quickly as possible.

Medium Risk MISPERS fall in-between.

As previously stated, the reason why the correct risk assessment is so important is that it dictates the action that investigators must take. For example in High Risk cases, a Police Search Advisor (PoLSA) *must* be contacted to give expert advice on where to search for that particular MISPER, the resources needed, e.g. officers, dogs, helicopter, etc.; whereas a PoLSA would not be requires for Low Risk MISPER Investigations.

Certain other tasks may be carried out depending on the risk level. These include such things as gathering local CCTV material, mobile phone information and records, house-to-house enquiries, searches of properties and open spaces, enquiries of family and friends, hospitals, GP's, banks, employers and fellow employees, educational establishments, carrying out leaflet drops and issuing regular press releases. The list is almost endless.

The reviewer's role is next to ensure that all necessary enquiries have been pursued expeditiously, and finally, to assess whether or not the deceased might have been found alive had investigators acted differently. In my experience, High Risk MISPERS who go on to take their own life, do so very soon after they disappear. Consequently, the chances of finding alive, a MISPER seriously intent on taking their own life, are usually quite low. In most cases they are already dead by the time they have been formally reported missing.

The following are examples of cases where Chief Officers had concerns about a particular MISPER investigation and ordered a review. The first is that of an elderly gentleman whose wife reported him missing from their seaside home. Police provided a really professional response. They searched the home and surrounding areas, mobilised the police helicopter, coastguard and lowland search teams. They made enquiries of the ambulance service and the local hospital; officers even managed to produce and distribute posters throughout the area. However, he seemed to have 'disappeared into thin air'. The MISPER was eventually traced to the local hospital mortuary!

Enquiries revealed that he had collapsed soon after leaving home, whilst cycling in the street. An ambulance had then conveyed him to hospital. Once there he was certified dead and taken to the mortuary. Yet repeated enquiries of the ambulance service and the hospital had failed to locate him.

In the end it was a call to the police by a member of the public that solved the mystery. She wanted to know what to do with the deceased's pedal cycle that had been removed to her garage for safe keeping!

I conducted a review of the police response, and, with their co-operation, I also reviewed ambulance service and hospital procedures.

It transpired that the MISPER was not carrying any identification when he collapsed. As he was still alive, or at least being resuscitated, and had not been involved in a road traffic collision, the police were not informed. Instead, an ambulance was called to the scene.

Members of the public removed his cycle for safekeeping and when the ambulance arrived the crew whisked him off to hospital. Unfortunately he was found to be dead on arrival so he was not actually taken into the Accident and Emergency (A & E) department. Instead a doctor came out to the ambulance to certify death and he was taken straight to the mortuary.

Again, unfortunately, A & E staff did not make a computer record of the fact that an unidentified male had been brought to their department, being primarily concerned with patients who had actually entered it.

The still unidentified deceased's arrival at the mortuary was manually documented, but no computer record was made. What also exacerbated the situation was the fact that it was late Friday afternoon and mortuary staff were about to leave work and would not normally be updating their computer records until the following Monday.

Consequently, when the police later made enquiries of the hospital, staff only checked their computer records and so could find no trace of his attendance either *in* A & E or at the mortuary.

A review of ambulance service records revealed that they had picked up a collapse case and had transported the unidentified patient to hospital. At no stage had his name been added to their incident record. Consequently, when police had enquired about a missing man, whose name was provided to them, they could find no matching patient.

Following meetings with senior staff at the A & E Department and the ambulance service, procedures were introduced to ensure that a similar situation could not re-occur. Police procedures were also updated so that if such mistakes were again made by the other services, there was a 'safety net' in place to alert them.

Another MISPER Found Dead Review was conducted after police dealt with a report of a man who had gone missing whilst en route to London where he worked. He was found dead the following day, behind his back garden fence! The review established that the man had been reported missing after failing to arrive at work. Initial police enquiries revealed that he had last been seen walking up the road towards his local underground station. Police obtained CCTV pictures of the station itself and found that he had arrived at the station to catch his train.

Not surprisingly, the police investigation then focussed on an examination of his normal route from the station to his workplace. No trace could be found of him so police eventually resumed their search from his home in case he had somehow found his way back without being seen. His body was then found.

Whilst one can understand the concerns about initial police action that had failed to find him earlier, but all the evidence indicated that he had disappeared en-route to work and there was nothing to suggest that he had actually disappeared whilst returning home.

Other things that had hampered the search included the fact that his body was found on an overgrown pathway behind his back garden fence, which led nowhere. It was never used by the MISPER or any other residents and was, therefore, almost the last place one would look.

Also, the back fence had been sited on a ridge raising it above ground level, Consequently, one would not have been able to see the other side of the fence without climbing on or over the fence; and there was no reason why anyone would ever look there.

The final example of a MISPER Found Dead Review relates to a woman who went missing from home, but was later found dead having hung herself in her back garden!

The review established that on the morning in question the MISPER, had been reported missing from home because her relatives had concerns about her mental health. Police were told that she had actually been heard leaving the house via the front door. Consequently they immediately focussed on a search of the local streets, parks and other open spaces. They wanted to intercept her before she got too far away.

They failed to locate her and on later attending her home, searched it and the garden, where her body was found. It appears that after walking out the front door, she double-backed into the garden, something that few, if any, could reasonably have anticipated.

Few such reviews have uncovered any serious negligence and as time has gone on, the police service has become much better at dealing with these incidents. But there are always lessons to be learnt; lessons that are then incorporated into MISPER policy and procedures.

CHAPTER 15
THE DISAPPEARANCE OF ROBIN PERRY & OTHERS

As previously stated, if person goes missing and their life is clearly at risk, the family expects a professional response from the police and the other emergency services.

When that response is not as expected they quite rightly want to know why. And if the explanations provided are inadequate or unsatisfactory, this can make them even more inquisitive; worse still they begin to suspect foul play, followed by a 'cover-up'. They then become even more determined to discover what really happened to their loved one, a determination that does not diminish during the following weeks, months, years or even decades.

The disappearance of Robin Perry is a case in point. In January 1969, Robin was a twenty four year-old father of two children, living with his wife in Southend-on-Sea, Essex. Around 3pm on Saturday 4th January 1969, Robin and five friends set out to go wildfowling on Ministry of Defence (MOD) land at Foulness Island, Essex. They travelled in two cars, driving past the War Department Constabulary's post at the entrance to the MOD's site, which was then known as the Proof and Experimental Establishment (PEE).

They drove to an area of Foulness Island known as the Wakering Stairs, got out of their cars and split into two, three-man parties, before walking out towards Havengore Creek. Robin's party also comprised Richard Pinch who was then aged twenty two, and twenty one year-old Andrew Bull.

It was low tide and strictly speaking they were trespassing, but they may not have known this as it was an area often frequented by other wildfowlers and dog walkers. Wildfowlers actually required licenses, issued by the MOD Superintendent.

Foulness Island itself has two small villages and the land is mainly farmed by locals. It is a restricted area, but there are certain rights of way across the island. These are suspended when red flags are flying as those flags denote the live firing of ammunition.

Maplin Sands covers an area of some thirty to forty square miles. When the tide is out the sands are mainly flat and firm, sloping gradually towards the sea for a distance of up to three miles. The MOD used the sands when test firing weapons and ammunition. When the tide turned, foreign shipping, including Russian vessels, would frequently anchor in the estuary. Wildfowlers could walk across the mudflats and get quite close to the ships; and presumably the seafarers could just as easily get close to land, via the mudflats. However, parts of the mudflats were separated by small channels up to ten feet deep. Some of those channels, also known as swingways, were always full of water, whilst others only filled with water when the tide came in.

It was around 4.45pm when a member of the other party, feeling cold, returned to the cars. The other two joined him around 5.30pm. By then the sea mist was rolling in and they became concerned for their companions. The three men went back to the sands and began shouting and firing their guns in the hope of guiding the three missing men back to land, but they failed to return.

Around 6.35pm, the trio went to the police post where they reported the men missing. They were advised to return to the Wakering Stairs and to shine their cars' headlamps out to sea, which they did. Soon, they were joined by a military Landover. The driver was asked to drive his vehicle onto the sands, but he refused to do so without the necessary authority.

A War Department Constabulary Inspector attended with a loud hailer. He was asked about any amphibious vehicles (known as DUKWS) and although one was available, it was not immediately deployed. In any event, amphibious vehicles would not usually be allowed onto the sands in fog, without radar. The Inspector was asked if the radar could be used, but allegedly said that it would be useless in these circumstances. Captain Collins (MOD) was later to say that the radar was manned by civilians who would have had to be called out from their homes to operate the equipment, which, in any event, would take time to warm up.

It was not until 8.45pm that the Essex County Constabulary was informed of the three men's disappearance, and two constables from Rochford Police Station arrived on the scene at 9.20pm.

At 9.50pm, well over three hours after the alarm had first been formally raised, the coastguard was informed and for a while the police and coastguard vehicles parked on the shore with their blue lights flashing.

During the next seventy two hours a thorough search of the area was carried out. Searchers included an RAF helicopter from Manston, more than thirty Essex County Constabulary officers, some with police dogs, a police launch, soldiers and dozens of family members and friends. Unfortunately, they failed to locate the missing men. The only significant find was that of Richard Pinch's combat jacket, which was found near the sea wall at Havengore Creek.

On the 20th March 1969, Richard Pinch's body was found on the outer edge of the sands. A post mortem examination found that he had drowned. Then, on the 26th June 1969, Andrew Bull's body was found by cockle fisherman. It was off-shore and partly embedded in the sands. The body had actually been there for several weeks. The fishermen who found him had previously seen something at that location, but had not realised it was a body. Only when their curiosity got the better of them did they make the gruesome discovery.

A post mortem examination was carried out and it was found that the body was low in saline. This suggested that Andrew had drowned in an area where fresh water runs from the island into the sea, rather than further out at sea. It also indicated that he had probably drowned early evening and before the tide came back in, perhaps in one of the swingways (channels). The Inquest into his death recorded a verdict of Accidental Death by drowning. Robin Perry's body has never been found.

The men's' disappearance was investigated by Essex County Constabulary. The investigating officer concluded that at some stage the three men had made their way seaward, mistaking beacons at the outer edge of the sands for shore lights. They then got into difficulties in a swingway causing Richard Pinch to discard his heavy combat jacket in order to stay afloat. Their bodies were later swept out into the estuary.

The families of the three men could not understand why an organised search involving the civil police, the coastguard and the lifeboat service had not begun far earlier than it had. The three men had been officially reported missing around 6.30pm and local people were later to say that it would be 9pm that night, before the sea would be high enough for them to drown in.

It seemed, therefore, that if the men had not earlier drowned in a swingway, they might still have been alive at 9pm. If so, they may have been found by the coastguard or lifeboat men, had those services been notified in time.

At the subsequent Inquest, the Coroner highlighted the need for better liaison between the War Department Constabulary and the civil police. Another outcome was that in future, the War Department Constabulary would ensure they were better equipped to deal with such incidents, in particular, with amphibious vehicles readily available. They would also carry out closer checks on people coming onto the island.

Robin's family still could not understand why his body had never been found and some wondered if the presence of Russian shipping in the area could be the key to this mystery. It was after all, the 'Cold War' period, a time when spies were allegedly secretly exchanged. They wondered if it was possible that Robin had stumbled across such an exchange and had paid for it with his life. It might, they reasoned, explain why the authorities had been slow to react and why they appeared to be so secretive.

There were other aspects of the case that the family found strange. For example, the radar was switched off that night, the men's guns were not found, the two bodies recovered were only found after major press coverage; and Robin's insurance was quickly paid out despite the fact that his body had not been found.

The families raised their concerns with the local Member of Parliament, Bernard (later Sir Bernard) Braine. He wrote to the Defence Secretary requesting details of the search and became concerned with what he later described as the '...inaccurate, misleading and evasive way in which the authorities have responded throughout to requests for information.' The MP cited a simple example.

He had requested details of the numbers of P&EE personnel involved in the search. He was initially told that it was between thirty and seventy. However, those figures were later corrected to between thirteen and seventy, figures later contradicted by the War Department Constabulary's Inspector who told the Inquest that he had only four men available to him that night!

The families and their MP continued to press the authorities for answers, often with little or no response. Eventually, on the 13th February 1970, Bernard Braine raised the matter in the House of Commons, the exchanges being documented in Hansard. Mr Braine recounted his and the families' experiences in trying to get to the bottom of what had happened the night the three men went missing.

Clearly frustrated he said, 'I have never known Ministers to behave in a more evasive, insensitive and myopic way as they have done in this case.' He called for an enquiry into the incident.

Mr Elystan Morgan, the Joint Under Secretary of State for the Home Department replied, refuting Mr Braine's allegations and refusing the request for a formal enquiry.

Mr Brain attempted to get further answers from Mr Morgan, but The Speaker adjourned the session.

This whole process served only to convince the families that there was far more to Robin's disappearance than the authorities were then prepared to admit, a view still strongly held by some surviving family members.

In a further attempt to establish exactly what had happened, the families employed a private detective, former Southend Inspector Archie Rickwood. He carried out a thorough investigation taking statements from all civilians who were on the island the day the three men went missing. He also interviewed local inhabitants familiar with the sands and their peculiarities and examined the evidence of the shots fired that day, contacting local wildfowlers and gun shops in the process. A reward for the recovery of the missing guns was also offered.

Mr Rickwood then obtained details of all thirty eight ships known to have been in the area that night, twenty of which had been quite close to the sands. One was a Russian ship. The captains and owners were all written to, but no useful information was obtained.

Mr Rickwood then looked at cases of drowning recorded in the local Coroner's records and examined charts and tide tables to see if he could work out how long it would take a body to wash ashore; but the results of those enquiries were inconclusive.

Nevertheless, as a result of all his investigations and the finding of the two bodies, Rickwood concluded that all three men had got lost and had subsequently drowned.

The case would not have come to my attention had Robin's daughter, Helen, not written to Essex Police requesting a copy of the original police report. The enquiry was subsequently referred to the Review Team, but due to the passage of time, the force no longer had a copy and she was informed accordingly.

Helen then wrote back sending me copies of various documents, including newspaper reports of the day and a copy of the Parliamentary debate as recorded in Hansard. She also said that her uncle Brian (Robin's brother) had met with Whitehall officials in 1971 when he was allegedly told that a 'D' Notice had been imposed. (A 'D' Notice, or Defence Advisory Notice, is an official request to news editors not to publish or broadcast items on specified subjects for reasons of national security.) The officials also allegedly told him that the true circumstances would only become clear in thirty years' time, the delay being due to the Official Secrets Act.

In addition to making enquiries of Essex Police, Helen had also contacted the Ministry of Defence requesting a copy of their file on the incident. Eventually she accessed it via the National Archive at Kew.

Having reviewed all available documents, including extracts from the original Ministry of Defence file, I am not convinced that there was anything suspicious about Robin's disappearance; or that the authorities, especially the police, tried to 'hush' anything up.

I say this because I also know that from time to time the police service, like many other large public sector organisation, gets things wrong. Unfortunately, on occasions, instead of quickly acknowledging those mistakes and apologising, we either say nothing or we try to justify something that cannot really be justified. Then, the more we are challenged about our response (or lack of response), the bigger the hole we dig when trying to extricate ourselves.

Records suggest that this incident was not properly dealt with from the outset. When someone goes missing in a misty environment within large coastal areas like Foulness Island and the Maplin Sands, it should never be assumed that they will probably find their way back to dry land unaided. The coastguard should have been informed when the three men were first reported missing. They would have co-ordinated a search of the sea and coastline which would probably have required the immediate deployment of lifeboats and sufficient numbers of properly trained and equipped police officers and other MOD personnel.

The fact that little effective searching was undertaken before 9pm probably meant that the chances of finding the men alive were significantly reduced. It also appears that the reason why little effective action was taken early on was due to the fact that, at that time, the civil police and the War Department Constabulary did not have joint protocols in place to cover such emergencies.

An early acknowledgement of our combined shortcomings, followed by an apology to the families, may have evaporated the air of suspicion surrounding this case and saved many years of heartache. But over forty years on, was there anything more that could now be done?

Every year the bodies of some of the people reported missing in the United Kingdom (UK) are found at locations in and around the UK (including the seas) sometimes as far afield as France and The Netherlands. Bearing in mind that record keeping and communications between European and UK police forces back in 1969, were not as good as they are today, might Robin's body have already been recovered far from Foulness, but the connection not made?

It might therefore be worthwhile re-examining old police records of unidentified bodies and body parts.

A full description of Robin Perry was compiled, including details of his clothing and any property believed to have been in his possession when he disappeared. The National Missing Persons Database (NMPD) was then searched. Most of the unidentified bodies recorded on the database could quickly be eliminated; but initially two could not.

The first was a body found in the English Channel on the 23rd August 1969. The other was found on a beach in The Netherlands on the 2nd November 1969. Enquiries were made via Interpol who contacted the police services of both countries. They searched their archives and having obtained further information about the recovered bodies, we were able to eliminate both as being Robin's body. For example, the body found in the Channel had only been in the water for about three months and unlike Robin, the deceased had had all his wisdom teeth extracted.

The National Missing Persons Bureau then identified a third possible case, that of the decomposed body of a man who had washed ashore in Lincolnshire on the 14th June 1969. The body, including the skull, teeth and jawbone, was photographed and a dental chart prepared. It was clear that the deceased had undergone significant dental work during his lifetime. A subsequent post mortem examination concluded that death was consistent with drowning and the body was buried soon after the post mortem examination.

However, on examining the archived records we found that the deceased appeared to be of a similar description to Robin, so an exhumation was considered. Our hope was that samples could be obtained from the remains that might then be used to develop his DNA profile. But first we had to exhaust all other possible methods of identification.

Unfortunately, we did not have Robin's dental chart, but according to his family, Robin's teeth were in good shape. Attempts were made to identify Robin's dentist via his National Health Service (NHS) medical card, but enquiries of the NHS revealed that his medical records were no longer in existence.

In the end, photographs of Robin, smiling, were obtained from the family and submitted to a forensic dentist (known as a Forensic Odontologist). He compared them with the photographs of the unidentified man's teeth and jawbone and concluded that they did not match. Also, the fact that, unlike the deceased, Robin had not had much dental work carried out on his teeth must have helped the Odontologist reach his final conclusions.

Nationally, further work by the National Missing Persons Bureau (NMPB) and forensic scientists saw the creation of a National Missing Persons DNA Database (NMPDNAD) which, as the name implies, is solely concerned with recording the DNA profiles of missing persons, plus the DNA profiles of unidentified bodies and body parts.

The DNA profiles of missing persons are now routinely developed and stored on the database, to be compared with the DNA of any unidentified bodies or body parts that may later be found.

The NMPB then begun an operation encouraging all police forces to look again at previously unidentified bodies or body parts found in their force areas. The aim was to see if scientific advances in DNA and fingerprint technology might finally lead to identifications.

As part of our on-going attempts to resolve Robin's disappearance, it was decided that we should request voluntary DNA samples from Robin's brother, sister and daughter and then see if their DNA profiles bore any similarities to the DNA profiles of any unidentified bodies or body parts now recorded on the NMPDNAD.

Robin's family readily agreed to provide DNA samples, but their subsequent DNA profiles did not provide a match to any already on the database. But they would now be routinely compared with the DNA profiles of any unidentified bodies or body parts that are subsequently added to this database.

More recently, we became aware of an unidentified decomposing body that had washed ashore near Redcar, in 1970.

The body had later been interred in the local cemetery.

Archived records revealed that a boot similar in size and style to one possibly worn by Robin the day he disappeared was found with the body, together with a fastened belt which was the same size as Robin's waist.

In due course the body was exhumed for a DNA sample to be obtained. This was profiled, but did not match the profiles provided by Robin's family. Though disappointing, that process may have increased the chances of police eventually identifying the Redcar body.

I very much hope that one day we will be able to locate Robin's body and prove his death was an accident, if only to bring peace of mind to his family.

Nationally, Hertfordshire Constabulary achieved an early success when new fingerprint technology enabled them to identify a woman who was killed crossing the M25 in Hertfordshire, in July 1990. Sadly, she died after being hit by several vehicles, but despite extensive enquiries and media appeals she was not identified.

Then, in 2010, fingerprints from the body were scanned and searched utilising modern fingerprint technology. As a result, the fatal accident victim was identified as a long term missing person, Lesley Ann Pickavance.

Police forces are still developing the DNA profiles of unidentified bodies and body parts recovered during the past few decades so that these can then be checked against missing persons' DNA profiles already on record. In order to do this they are trying to recover any remaining biological samples taken during the original post mortem examinations and if necessary, by exhuming the bodies themselves.

In addition, where review officers uncover a possible name for an unidentified body, blood relatives can be approached (as Robin's family was) and asked to provide kinship DNA samples for DNA profiling. Their DNA profiles can then be compared with the DNA profile of the previously unidentified body. This was something we considered when reviewing the disappearance of a man who was reported missing in the summer of 1980.

Cyril Thorpe was a forty four year-old unemployed site agent who lived with his partner Marian, on a houseboat moored at West Mersea, Essex.

On the 31st July that year, Cyril was seen sailing his dingy down the River Blackwater. He failed to return that day and police launched a search for him which later became a missing person's investigation. Five days later Cyril's dingy was found drifting, but there was no sign of him. Cyril's disappearance attracted a great deal of media attention at the time. His brother Roy and sister Joyce travelled to Essex to assist television companies covering the story. Sadly, he was not found.

Then, on the 22nd December 1980, the badly decomposed body of a man was found on the beach at the Colne Nature Reserve at St Osyth. Marine Police Officers studied charts of the river and realised that this could be the body of Cyril Thorpe. The pathologist who carried out the post mortem examination looked at the description of Cyril which police had been given and could not exclude the possibility that this was indeed him. Disappointing, due to the state the body was in, no formal identification was possible and the remains were eventually buried in an un-named grave in Clacton Cemetery.

Many years later, when the NMPB were encouraging police forces to look again at previously unidentified bodies found in their force areas, they provided all forces with a list of such cases. The list they supplied to Essex Police included the body found at St Osyth. Police and Coroner's files were recovered and the case reviewed.

We soon realised that there might now be an opportunity to finally establish whether or not the body found at St Osyth was indeed that of Cyril Thorpe. If his brother and sister could be traced, voluntary DNA samples could be requested of them and DNA profiles obtained. The body could then be exhumed and a DNA sample obtained and profiled. All these profiles could then be compared and it might now be possible to confirm or otherwise, that the unidentified body and Cyril Thorpe's siblings were biologically related to each other.

Our first task was to trace Cyril's brother and sister. However, this might be difficult as we did not know the sister's surname, their current addresses or dates of birth. Coroner's records from thirty years ago revealed that in 1980, Cyril's brother Roy was living at an address in Pinchbeck, Lincolnshire.

I arranged for Lincolnshire Police to make enquiries at the address and they found that Roy had long since moved away without leaving any forwarding address. They expanded their enquiries, but could not trace him.

The Coroner's file also showed that Cyril's father was living at an address in St Albans Road West, in Hatfield, Hertfordshire. Unfortunately, enquiries revealed that the address no longer existed. Cyril's sister was our only hope.

Research was carried out by one of our intelligence officers, Jenny. From Cyril's birth certificate she established that his mother's maiden name was Devine. Jenny carried out further searches for any other children born between 1930 – 1950, whose father's surname was Thorpe and whose mother's name was Thorpe nee Devine.

Five names emerged. The first three were born in Lancashire so were least likely to be related to Cyril. The remaining two were Roy and Joyce Thorpe who were both born in Surrey. Further checks revealed that Roy Thorpe had probably died in 1984 and that his sister had married her husband Frederick in St Albans, Hertfordshire in 1961. They were both now living in Kent.

I anticipated that a visit from a Kent Police officer who had little knowledge of the case might be upsetting, so in November 2012, I drove to Joyce's home taking with me a voluntary DNA sampling kit. I knocked on the door and after introducing myself, Joyce's husband invited me in. Joyce then joined us and I explained that we were re-investigating the death of a man whose body had been found on a beach in Essex, in December 1980. I told her we were aware of the fact that her brother Cyril had gone missing in the same area some months before and were trying to determine if the body was that of Cyril.

'It won't be him.' She said confidently.

I had to tread carefully. Some people have great difficulty in finally coming to terms with the death of a loved one.

'No. It's definitely not Cyril.'

'How can you be so sure?'

'Because he phoned me up nine years after he went missing.'

She then went on to explain that one day Cyril had telephoned her 'out of the blue'. He told her he had received a knock on the head and had lost his memory. But Joyce did not really believe him. According to his sister, Cyril was a 'man of mystery' who was always up to something and would go for years without contacting any members of his family.

Joyce went on to tell me a little about her brother's activities over the years and it appeared to me that some of the things he had told his family were indeed, quite fanciful.

Apparently, Cyril had concluded his last telephone conversation with Joyce by saying that he might pop round one day when he was in the area.

She's still waiting; and what happened to him after that call is unknown.

We have still not identified the body found at St Osyth, but of one thing we can be sure; it is not Cyril Thorpe.

When it comes to identifying long-standing unidentified bodies, perhaps our best result to date has been in formally identifying the dead body of a partially clothed woman who was found on the foreshore at Foulness Island on 16th April 2000. The woman appeared to be around forty five years of age, but there was nothing on or about her body that might help police identify her.

The initial investigation was carried out by Essex Police as the cause of death was unknown and could therefore have been suspicious. Fortunately, the following day a post mortem examination revealed that the cause of death was immersion, with no evidence of foul play.

Consequently, the death was deemed non-suspicious and the investigation handed over to the Ministry of Defence (MOD) Police since it was on their land that the body had been found. The body was routinely fingerprinted, but when searched on the National Fingerprint Database it came back as 'no trace'. It appeared that she was not known to the police. The MOD Police widely publicised the case and carried out extensive enquiries, but the woman could not be identified.

On the 27th September 2000, at Southend Coroner's Court, an 'Open' verdict was recorded and after a simple ceremony, the body was interred in an un-named grave in Hall Road Cemetery at Rochford .

In July 2012, more than twelve years after the body had been found, a family living in London contacted the City of London Police. They formally reported a family member, 'Margaret Whitely' (not her real name) missing. It appears that 'Margaret' had led a somewhat nomadic existence, sometimes going for many years without contacting her family. Interestingly, they had last heard from her in the year 2000, when she was living in a Southend hotel.

The City Police asked their Essex colleagues to do some local enquiries, but the hotel where 'Margaret' had last stayed could not be identified. However, enquiries revealed that 'Margaret' was already known to the police having been arrested during the 1990's for a couple or relatively minor matters. Her fingerprints had then been taken so she was already on the National Fingerprint Database.

Unfortunately, though her PNC record provided details of her arrests in the 1990's and her description, it contained little else. Certainly her fingerprints had not later been linked to any unidentified bodies or body parts recovered from around the UK during the last decade or so (including the Foulness body).

The City Police were unable to take their missing person's investigation any further, but in November, a member of the same family contacted the National Missing Persons Bureau (NMPB) to say she was 99% certain that an e-fit of the Foulness body, which had just been published on the NMPB website, was her aunt, 'Margaret Whitely'.

The enquiry was passed to our team as Home Office procedures had changed; it was now the responsibility of the county force to resolve such matters, rather than the MOD.

An expert from the National Fingerprint Bureau directly compared the fingerprints taken from 'Margaret Whitely' in the 1990's with those taken from the Foulness body; and they matched. Asked why they had not been identified back in 2000, the expert said that one of the reasons was the poor quality of the fingerprints of the dead body.

Having previously worked at seaside towns, I knew that bodies washed ashore often had wrinkled fingers, known as 'washer-woman's hands', and that these are difficult to fingerprint and scan into a computer. However, a direct comparison by a fingerprint expert, of the fingerprint records of a dead body and those of a known criminal, is more likely to be successful. But to do this police always need a possible name to work with.

I arranged for the identification to be confirmed by an Essex Police fingerprint expert who confirmed her colleague's identification.

I then made enquiries of Rochford District Council who gave me the exact location of the un-named grave. I visited the graveyard and found the grave marked by a plain wooden cross. I photographed it and sent a copy of the photograph to 'Margaret's' family, by text. Their search was over.

I provided details of the council official with whom they should liaise regarding the erection of a headstone. I also made further enquiries and spoke to the priest who had conducted the original burial. He offered to conduct a memorial service for the family, so I passed his contact details to them.

But the unidentified body had first to be legally registered in her real name. In due course, I provided a report to H M Coroner and gave oral evidence of the identification by fingerprints. The Coroner then swore an affidavit which was subsequently submitted to the Registrar of Births, Marriages and Deaths, who then amended the original death certificate.

This was the first time that a missing person had been provisionally identified by a family using the search facility on the NMPB's Website.

This case should give some hope to relatives of long term MISPERS that their disappearance may eventually be resolved even though it may take many years.

CHAPTER 16
THE RAPE AND MURDER OF KIM ROBERTS

In 1964, the east end of London was still recovering from the ravages of the Second World War. Areas like Stepney comprised a combination of new council houses, older buildings, 'prefabs' (prefabricated homes) and bomb sites.

This environment was home to seven year-old Kim Roberts. She lived with her parents Joe and Pat, two brothers and a sister, in a maisonette in Stepney Way. This street ran between the Mile End Road and Commercial Road.

Two or three years before her disappearance, Kim had been accosted so knew not to speak to strangers.

Following Sunday lunch on the 1st March 1964, Kim, dressed in her school uniform, went out into the street to play with friends. She was last seen by her parents around 5pm.

There were several sightings of Kim during the next hour or so, the last one being around 6pm when she was seen talking to a man cleaning his car.

Kim failed to return home as promised by 6.30pm, so her father went out looking for her. Unable to find Kim, Mr Roberts reported her missing just after 8pm and a full scale search was mounted by the local police. But the investigation was soon taken over by Detective Superintendent Axon of Scotland Yard. Kim appeared to have vanished into thin air.

Then, around 2 pm on Wednesday 4th March 1964, two boys out looking for dumped radios, found the clothed body of a young girl lying in Watts Wood, Purfleet, Essex. This location, popular with courting couples, was just off what was once the main A13 road from London to Southend-on-Sea, and about fifteen miles from Stepney Way.

Detective Superintendent Axon drove to the crime scene where he was joined by Essex detectives, led by the then Head of Essex CID, Detective Chief Superintendent Jack Barkway. They were joined by a Home Office Pathologist and a joint Metropolitan Police and Essex County Constabulary major crime investigation was launched.

The girl's body was removed to the local mortuary where she was identified by her father as Kim Roberts. A post mortem examination revealed that Kim had been raped and strangled. The pathologist opined that Kim's death was likely to have occurred within six hours of her last meal. If that was her Sunday lunch (which Kim had eaten around 2.30pm) then she was probably already dead when police had first begun their search for her. Enquiries at the scene led police to believe that the body may have lain undiscovered since Sunday evening.

On the Sunday Kim disappeared, there were various sightings of men and vehicles in the area around her home and at Watts Wood. In fact, a motorist told police that around the time Kim's body was thought to have been dumped, he saw a man in what he believed was an Austin A50 saloon car parked a few yards from the track where her body was later found. The man, he said, was lifting what looked like a large parcel out of the car's boot. The motorist challenged him and was told to 'clear off'. Police were given a description, but he was never traced.

The murder attracted national publicity with the Sunday Mirror offering a £2,000 reward, a significant sum in 1964. During the following months hundreds of possible witnesses and known suspects were interviewed and over 5,000 statements taken; but the killer was never caught.

For the next few decades, the case lay fairly dormant. Then, on the 15th June 2004, the investigation was unexpectedly re-opened. Essex Police was contacted by a man enquiring about the possible murder of a child named Kim Roberts many years before. He told police that the previous afternoon his step-father Robert, had confessed to the killing, but the caller did not know whether or not to believe him.

The man explained that he had gone to his mother's home in Laindon, Essex, for Sunday dinner. As she prepared their meal, he went to the local pub for a drink with his step-father. In due course they returned home for dinner and it was then that Robert allegedly broke down in tears before confessing to a murder. He told them that he had strangled a girl named Kim Roberts and had dumped her body in the grass at Purfleet; then said that he had taken her because he wanted someone to have sex with.

Later that afternoon, having composed himself, Robert went to sleep.

That evening members of the family discussed the confession amongst themselves. None of them had ever heard of the Kim Roberts murder; the girl's name meant nothing to them. Bravely, they decided that the police should be informed the next day and the officers would have to take whatever action they deemed necessary.

Enquiries commenced and on the 18th June 2004, Robert was arrested by detectives from Stanway Major Investigations Team (MIT) led by Detective Superintendent Gareth Wilson. His house was thoroughly searched, but nothing of any significance was found.

Robert was interviewed at length and he did not deny having confessed to the murder. However, he denied having killed Kim Roberts and could not explain why he had confessed to it. Robert was released on police bail pending the outcome of various enquiries. These included locating the original case material and exploring any possible forensic opportunities such as DNA.

Enquiries revealed that the original forensic work had been carried out at the Metropolitan Police Forensic Science Laboratory; but unfortunately, forty years, on the case material was no longer available.

The MIT, having completed most of their enquiries, then contacted the Review Team for an urgent review of their investigation to be carried out. At that time their main questions were what should be done when the suspect answered bail? Should he be arrested? Could he be arrested and interviewed further? If so, what questions should be put to him?

I attended a briefing at the MIT office and left still mystified as to why this suspect had made such an apparently unsolicited confession in the first place. Prior to his confession, there had been no recent publicity about the Kim Robert's murder and there seemed no obvious 'trigger' for the confession.

True, there had been some publicity about the newly formed Major Crime Review Team and about 'Cold Case' reviews generally. So had Robert seen that publicity and if so, did he now feel that his past was about to catch up with him?

It also puzzled me that Robert had not simply confessed to killing *a* child; he had actually named the child concerned. If he knew nothing about the murder, where did he get the name Kim Roberts from?

I was also intrigued by the fact that in 1964, he was living in Benfleet, Essex, but working in Silvertown, which like Kim's home, is also in the east end of London. Since he used to drive to and from work, the most direct route would have been along the old A13, taking him to within 'spitting distance' of Watts Wood, Purfleet. Robert also worked some weekends so may well have worked the Sunday that Kim disappeared.

We began the review by reading all the statements and other documents either recovered or generated by the MIT. We discovered that whilst detectives had identified Robert's previous employers and the general locations where he had worked in the 1960's, they appeared not to have established exactly where his man was working in March 1964. So how close was his workplace to Stepney Way; and would his normal route home from work have actually taken him past that road or Watts Wood?

I felt that he could and should be rearrested even his detention 'clock' was running out. However, if detectives wished to continue their questioning, they would have to put Robert before the magistrates court for a Warrant of Further Detention.

There were a number of things that in my view, could be done to progress the investigation, plus matters that could be put to him during further interviews. I set these out in a report and within an interview plan. In particular, I recommended that Robert (and his solicitor if he required it) should be driven from the police station to his former Benfleet home. He should then be driven towards the east end of London directing officers along the route he used to travel and then show them the exact location of his former workplace. Robert should then direct them back along the route he used to take to his former home.

That way, his routes to and from work could be firmly established. Also, detectives would then be able to see exactly where his workplace and thus the beginning of his route home were in relation to Kim's home and Watts Woods.

On arrival at both locations he should then be asked if he had ever been to Stepney Way or Watts Wood before; if so, when; and more importantly, why?

The journey would have to be videoed so as to accurately record the route and anything said by or to him. The trip would clarify certain things and may even provide further circumstantial evidence. I also felt that such a trip might help improve the rapport that now existed between Robert and the detectives who had been interviewing him.

It is a strange thing, but in my experience not all criminals are completely without a conscience. Some reach the stage when they would like to admit their wrongdoing, even if it means having to face the consequences, Investigators, therefore, should not make it unduly difficult for them to do so.

I remember once interviewing a man who had seriously sexually assaulted his two year-old daughter. He was, quite rightly, ashamed of what he had done and it really troubled him to the extent that I was sure he wanted to tell us exactly what he had done. If we had shown our natural revulsion of his actions he may not have felt able to talk to us about what he had done. Instead, we treated him with courtesy and he made a full confession even though he knew it would undoubtedly lead to his imprisonment, which it did.

Assuming the confession was true, I wondered if Robert may have been similarly troubled. He was a churchgoer and if, like me, he believed he would one day have to face his maker, he would probably not wish to do so without already having confessed and atoned for his wrongdoings. Robert was now seventy six years-old and not in the best of health. Perhaps he realised that he was in 'God's Waiting Room' and really needed to confess and to accept his punishment for raping and murdering this poor child.

If that was what he wished and if that wish had prompted the surprise confession he made to his family, then we should not make it any more difficult for him do so again. Further interviews would give him the opportunity to finally face up to his crimes.

The report and recommendations were forwarded to the Senior Investigating Officer (SIO) for consideration. In due course, the SIO decided not to arrest and interview Robert when he answered bail. Instead, investigations would continue and if any further evidence was forthcoming, he would then be re-arrested and further interviewed. He was therefore released from bail and informed that no further action would be taken against him; at least for the time being.

These are always difficult decisions for any SIO because to some extent they are dammed if they arrest, but get no-where; and dammed if they don't.

Unfortunately, no fresh evidence was forthcoming so this suspect was not re-arrested or further interviewed by the police.

However, our suspect was soon identified and actually named by the media; and an enterprising journalist was only too happy to drive both Robert and his wife to Purfleet and then to publish an account of their trip in the London Evening Standard. It was in September 2004, that Robert and his wife got into the journalist's car en-route to Purfleet. Robert said he wanted to see the woods where Kim's body was found.

'Why do you want to go there?' asked his wife. 'Do you think it might jog your memory?'

There was a silence; then Robert told his wife that he had never met or murdered Kim Roberts.

She told the reporter that she did not believe her husband and that she had found his request to be taken to the scene bizarre. They later separated and Robert moved away from the area.

The case remains un-solved; but if Robert was the killer, I hope that one day he finds the courage to face up to his crimes, but this time with a full confession to the police. That is the only way that Kim's family can finally lay her to rest.

CHAPTER 17
THE MURDER OF IVY KEMP

It was 7.15am on Monday 28th October 1968, when Kenneth Durrant got out of the bed he shared with his wife, Margaret. He wandered out onto the landing and noticed his landlady's bedroom door was open. This was unusual so he gingerly looked into the bedroom, not wishing to disturber her if she was still asleep. He stepped back in horror. The bedroom had been ransacked and Ivy Kemp lay dead in bed, the victim of a ferocious knife attack.

Ivy Lillian Kemp was a sixty nine year-old widow, who lived in a modern, three bedroomed detached house in New Century Road, Laindon, a suburb of Basildon New Town. Until relatively recently, Ivy had been quite active. But her health was beginning to fail and she had become a semi-invalid, spending much of her time in bed. Ivy owned a number of caravans that she let out to builders and labourers working close by. She also took in lodgers, which at that time included the Durrants and another man, William Dillon.

Police were called and a murder investigation was launched. In those days the importance of scene preservation had not yet been fully appreciated; and the crime scene log disclosed that 'the world and his wife' had visited the scene, including the Chief Constable of Essex!

The eminent Home Office Pathologist, Professor Francis Camps, also attended in order to examine the body whilst it was still in situ. He found that Ivy had suffered multiple stab wounds and holes in the bedclothes indicated that she had probably been stabbed whilst laying down in bed. No weapon was found either in or within the vicinity of the house. Subsequent tests found no evidence of a sexual assault and there appeared to be no clear motive for the attack. The house was found to be insecure; a ground floor room had its fanlight window open and the back door was not locked.

Mr and Mrs Durrant were interviewed. They told police that they had been out the previous day, returning home around 11.15pm.

They then watched television for a while before retiring to bed. Both said that when they went upstairs, Ivy was still awake and they said goodnight to her. Mrs Durrant told police that she had heard noises during the night which she could not really describe. But she did not wake her husband, nor did she investigate the noises herself.

The other lodger, William Dillon, was actually in Southern Ireland on the night the murder was committed and his alibi was confirmed by the local Garda Siochana (Southern Ireland Police).

Numerous documents were found in Ivy's bedroom, all of which were examined for fingerprints. Many fingerprints were recovered from those documents and from elsewhere inside the house, not all of which were identified.

Detectives spent many months investigating this murder, conducting numerous searches, house-to-house enquiries, interviewing witnesses and local suspects; all to no avail. Finally the investigation wound down pending any further developments.

The case lay dormant for a number of years, but in August 1984, a local paper gave further publicity to this still unsolved murder. As a direct result of that publicity, a local woman contacted police naming a local man who had allegedly confessed the murder to her. She also said the man had since died. A short witness statement was taken from her, but the officer then appears simply to have filed it with the case paper, probably because the suspect named was now dead.

In 2002, the National Automated Fingerprint Identification System (NAFIS) identified a previously unidentified fingerprint that had been found on one of the documents in Ivy's bedroom. It belonged to a convicted thief 'John Smith' (not his real name).

As this identification pre-dated the establishment of the Major Crime Review Team, it was passed to Brentwood Major Investigations Team (MIT) to follow up. But due to the more urgent demands of other investigations, it was not immediately followed up. It was then re-allocated to the newly formed Major Crime Review Team.

We examined the case material, but could find no evidence of 'John Smith' having come into the original enquiry.

A copy of the document upon which the fingerprint had been found was obtained; it was a letter sent to Ivy by an insurance company based in the City of London. 'John Smith' (now deceased) was then researched and on checking his record of employment, it was found that he had worked in the insurance industry around the relevant time, and had actually been based in the City of London. He had no record of violence and no known connections with Essex.

I concluded that the most likely explanation for his fingerprints being found on a document in Ivy's bedroom was that he had handled the letter whilst it was in the insurance company's office and before it had been posted to Ivy. In any event, that line of enquiry could not be pursued any further.

Nevertheless, the review had then discovered the information about alleged confession, which clearly warranted more attention than it had been given in 1984.

In her statement, the witness who had come forward in 1984, alleged that a week after Ivy's murder, a man she named had confessed the murder to her. (As relatives of the man are still alive and are unaware of the alleged confession, his real name has not been used. I will instead call him 'Bert'.) The witness went on to say that she had been out with her husband (who had also since died) when they met 'Bert' in the street. They both knew him as he used to frequent the same pubs and social clubs as they did.

Having confessed the murder, 'Bert' went on to explain why he had committed it. 'Bert' told her that he had previously borrowed money from Ivy and had gone to see her again as he wished to borrow some more. But Ivy refused to give him any more money and an argument ensued '... and that's why I did her over.'

The witness did not tell the police about 'Bert's' confession at the time; she was a member of a close knit community and in those days they did not talk to the police. But 'Bert' had since died so she had felt able to go to the police.

I researched the case papers and discovered that 'Bert' was one of many men interviewed during the original investigation. At the time he lived just a short distance away from Ivy. I obtained his full details and made further enquiries that confirmed he had died in the mid 1970's.

The case file showed that when routinely interviewed by murder squad detectives 'Bert' had told them that he knew Ivy quite well and had visited her in her bedroom, on a number of occasions. 'Bert' told detectives that the last time he saw Ivy was a week before the murder. Significantly, he told them that he had previously borrowed money from her, which he was still repaying.

When asked about his movements at the relevant time, 'Bert' told detectives that on the Sunday (the day before the murder) he had taken his wife and their young children to visit relatives in Southend-on-Sea. He went on to say that they had all returned home before midnight; and that he did not go out again.

I looked for an alibi statement from his wife, but found none. Fortunately, there was a report from a woman police officer who had interviewed 'Bert's' wife at the time. She had confirmed most of her husband's account of his movements that night. But it was clear that she had gone to bed before her husband and had soon fallen asleep. Consequently, he could easily have gone out again without her knowing. He need not have been gone long as Ivy only lived round the corner.

Interestingly, she ('Bert's' wife) knew of his association with Ivy and although she had no evidence to show that he was being unfaithful, 'Bert's' wife told the officer it would not have surprised her if he had had a sexual relationship with Ivy, despite Ivy's age and infirmity.

Because of what 'Bert' and his wife had told the police, forensic science was unlikely to be of much assistance, even if we could now develop 'Bert's' DNA profile. Similarly, if his fingerprints were found in Ivy's bedroom, they could easily be explained away by the fact that 'Bert' had previously visited Ivy on a number of occasions and may even have had a sexual relationship with her; at least that is what could have been argued on his behalf.

The only possible way forward was to re-interview 'Bert's' wife about her husband's movements that night; assuming she was still alive. Their children were probably too young to remember what, if anything, had happened that night.

I thought it was possible that 'Bert's' wife knew more about this murder than she had originally told the police; that she may have alibied her husband out of fear of violence, or a misplaced sense of loyalty. Might she give a different account now that he was dead?

Enquiries revealed that 'Bert's' wife was indeed still alive and I traced her to sheltered accommodation in London. She had remarried following 'Bert's' death, but was now a widow once again.

Detectives from Brentwood MIT visited her, but unfortunately, she refused to co-operate with them. And if this strong willed woman had covered for 'Bert' in 1968, she was certainly not about to inform on him now.

So what had the review achieved? Firstly, we were able to satisfactorily eliminate the person who had left a previously unidentified fingerprint at the murder scene.

Secondly, we had also discovered an important statement that had not previously been followed up; and by researching the case material had established that the suspect named therein had been interviewed by detectives at the time of the murder and that he had both the motive and opportunity to kill Ivy. He also had a rather shaky alibi!

Overall this was a disappointing result, but sometimes these cases are not solved outright and by re-examining them some further progress towards an eventual resolution is often made.

CHAPTER 18
THE IVY DAVIES MURDER

Ivy Lilian Davies was forty nine years-old when she was murdered. For many years she ran the Orange Tree Café (presently known as The Barge) on Westcliff-on-Sea's Western Esplanade, less than a mile from the world famous Southend Pier. Ivy's café was one of a terrace of cafés each of which had been built into what at first sight appears to be a row of railway arches. However, this row of arches actually sits below Shorefield Road, a street that rises upwards from the seafront towards the cliff top.

That particular area is not as open or as picturesque as the cliffs on the eastern side of the nearby Cliffs Pavilion. This is probably because during the nineteenth and twentieth centuries, hundreds of houses, shops and other business premises were built on the streets that lead from the main London Road towards the seafront. Most of those buildings remain today, although some of the more imposing dwellings have been converted into multi-occupancy dwellings, now in various states of repair.

The Orange Tree Café was a fairly typical Southend seafront café. It would open early in the morning, serving breakfasts to local fishermen and bait diggers. For the rest of the day and often into the evening, it would provide snacks and meals to local residents, trades people and tourists.

Ivy, a divorcee, lived alone in a small house in nearby Holland Road. Her two story house had once been a stable. She had a number of grown up children all of whom stayed in contact with her and with each other. Ivy's daily routine was fairly predictable. She would open her café first thing in the morning and would remain there for most of the day. Ivy employed a number of part time staff to help run the café and at the end of the day she would cash up, lock up and then walk the short distance to her home. Once home Ivy would often get out of her work clothes and relax in her dressing gown for the evening.

The evening of Monday 3rd February 1975, was no different. Being winter-time, the café did not usually stay open during the evening so it was around 6pm when Ivy locked the café up and walked home.

Around 10am the following morning, staff, including one of Ivy's daughters (also named Ivy) arrived at the café to find it was still locked up. They went to Ivy's house, let themselves in with a spare key and found her dead on the lounge floor. She had sustained head injuries and a ligature was round her neck although this had not been tied up tightly.

Police were informed and a murder enquiry was launched. Ivy was wearing her dressing gown, but this did not necessarily mean that she had just been going to bed when she was murdered.

A post mortem examination was carried out by Home Office Pathologist Professor James Cameron. He concluded that death had probably occurred two hours either side of midnight.

Police found no sign of a forced entry to the house, so had Ivy let her killer in? Furthermore, nothing appeared to be missing, so what was the motive for the attack?

A search of the house led to the discovery of Snap-On-Tool, known as a 20/50 pry bar, not far from her body. This had minute traces of blood thereon and this was later found to match Ivy's blood group. It was therefore deemed to be the murder weapon. This tool became the focus of the investigation and hundreds of owners of such tools were traced and interviewed. Those living in the Southend area and who were able to produce them to the police, were eliminated from the enquiry.

During the course of the investigation, nearly one thousand statements were taken and a number of local men arrested and interviewed; but the killer was never identified.

In 2004, Crimestoppers contacted Essex Police offering enhanced rewards for information relating to ten of Essex Police's most serious unsolved 'Cold Cases'. The Ivy Davies murder was selected as one of those that would be the subject of a fresh media appeal.

During the months following the media appeal a trickle of information was received, but it did not prove to be of any significance. However, all that was about to change.

On the 5th February 2005, I was off duty and received a telephone call from one of Ivy's relatives. He told me that he had been given the name of the person who had allegedly killed Ivy, a man who I will call 'George Anderson' although that is not his real name. I asked him where this information had come from and he gave me a name of a woman who I shall refer to as 'Vi', and her contact telephone number.

I returned home and telephoned 'Vi' who seemed quite happy to talk to me. She confirmed the name I had been given and gave me some background on 'George'. She also outlined what had allegedly happened on the night of the murder. If true, her account explained why no suspects had been seen that night. I asked 'Vi' how she knew all this and she told me it had come from a close personal friend who I will refer to as 'Angie', though once again, that is not her real name. 'Vi' would not give me 'Angie's' name or any contact details, so I encouraged 'Vi' to get 'Angie' to ring me. We needed to know where 'Angie' had obtained the information from in order to assess how reliable it may be.

Shortly after our conversation, 'Angie' did indeed telephone me. Rather frustratingly, she refused to give her name, address and telephone number, which had been withheld. She did, however, confirm what I had been told.

I spent some time trying to persuade 'Angie' to give me her name and contact details so I could visit her. But she repeatedly refused. Eventually she hung up. It was vitally important that 'Angie' was identified and interviewed 'face-to-face'. Unfortunately, I did not know who she was or where she lived; but I knew that we should be able to identify and trace her from telephone records of calls made to my home.

I returned to work and researched the Ivy Davies case papers. I discovered that all the individuals referred to during the earlier telephone conversations had been interviewed during the original investigation. They had all denied any knowledge of, or involvement in, Ivy's murder. They had also accounted for their movements on the night of the murder, but detectives had been unable to confirm all their stories. Nevertheless, there had been nothing connecting them to the Ivy Davies murder so no further action had been taken against them.

The re-investigation was passed to Rayleigh Major Investigations Team (MIT) then led by Detective Superintendent Simon Dinsdale. They began the mammoth task of tracing and interviewing the original witnesses, including 'Vi' and 'Angie'; and reviewing all the fingerprint and other forensic evidence.

On the 15th November 2005, 'George' was arrested and interviewed about Ivy's murder, which he denied. He was bailed whilst further enquiries were carried out. In the end there was no forensic or other evidence to link him to the murder, so he was released from bail and no further action was taken against him.

From time to time, further information is received and investigated in the hope that one day the case will be resolved. For example, in 2011 a man contacted the family saying that he knew Ivy, but had never been interviewed by the police. He was able to describe the inside of Ivy's house and said she used to keep large sums of money in her oven.

The man was traced and interviewed by detectives, but it transpired that he had ceased his contact with Ivy some considerable time before she was killed and had no useful information to contribute.

After the arrest of 'George', Ivy (Junior) spoke about what it was like not knowing who her mother's killer was. She said, 'It's something which never leaves you, because you never know if you're talking to the person who did it. It's forever there. At one time I thought it had to be someone I knew. Every knock at the door, I thought this might be the person. It takes a long time to come to terms with the shock of that.' Tragically Ivy (Junior) has also since died, but Ivy Davies' family, especially her son Victor, continue to seek justice for Ivy.

Quite recently he said, 'I feel like there's too many opportunities that have been let slip, but you never know. It's never too late, unless you get a deathbed confession – that's when it becomes too late … (but) it's too late for justice. What are they going to do? Throw away the key for what has got to be an old person now anyway?'

He continued, 'I just want to know why. I believe there are still people in the local community who know exactly what happened and why, not least those involved. They need to face up to what they did; or what they continue to do in shielding a killer. Let's hope that one day they will find the courage to do the right thing.'

CHAPTER 19
THE LAINDON RAPES

As previously stated, it is an unfortunate fact of life that rape is mostly committed by men who know their victims. Rapists will usually be family members, friends or acquaintances of the victim; or at least people that the victim has met before, albeit briefly, perhaps in a club, disco or at some other social gathering.

By contrast, rape committed by complete strangers is relatively rare, albeit that it is the crime that women most fear. But in reality it is just as frightening and degrading to be raped by someone you know as it is by a stranger. It is such a despicable act.

During the early 1990's a series of 'Stranger Rapes' occurred at Laindon, on the outskirts of Basildon. They were committed by a man the press dubbed 'The Laindon Rapist'. How many attacks he committed is not really known. Some victims do not report the attacks upon them; others do, but for a variety of reasons, investigators do not always link the crime to a particular series of attacks. It may be, for example, that the attack occurred at a location outside the area in which a particular rapist has previously operated; or perhaps his method of attack (MO – Modus Operandi) is different; or descriptions of the attacker may be significantly different.

However, there often comes a time when detectives realise that a particular attack is probably part of a series; and they may later confirm this via the suspect's DNA profile.

The 'Laindon Rapes' are thought to have started early 1990. Shortly after 4pm on the 19th March that year, two teenage girls were walking home from school, along a road that was then under construction and designated 'Road 50'. This is now believed to be Mandeville Way, Laindon.

Suddenly, a man in a stocking mask jumped out from the bushes, threatening them with a Stanley craft knife. He committed a serious indecent assault on one of the girls, who was then aged sixteen years, before running off.

The police were called and an investigation was launched, but the attacker was never identified.

The next attack occurred around 5.30pm on the 27th March 1990, a week after the first attack. Two sixteen year-old schoolgirls were walking along Laindon's semi-rural Lee Chapel Lane, when a man in a stocking mask jumped out from the bushes, threatening them with a Stanley craft knife. He forced them to undress, tied them up and committed serious sexual assaults on both. The police were called and an investigation launched; but again the attacker was not identified.

For a while, the attacker appeared to 'lie low', but around 3.30pm on the 8th October 1990, he struck again; and on the same road as his first victim i.e. 'Road 50'. This time the victim was a twenty year-old woman who was threatened by a stocking-masked man armed with a Stanley craft knife. The attacker indecently assaulted, then raped his victim.

By now, detectives were convinced they were dealing with a serial offender, but despite a major investigation, they failed to identify the attacker.

Once again, the rapist appeared to 'lie low' and it was not until 13th December 1991, that he is believed to have attacked again. An eighteen year-old woman was crossing a car park opposite a petrol station in Nethermayne, Basildon, when she was attacked by a man believed to be armed with a Stanley craft knife. He tore her skirt and committed an indecent assault, before running off with her handbag.

Again, detectives failed to identify her attacker.

What was thought to have been the last attack in that series occurred some nine months later. Around 6.30 am on the 14th August 1992, a fifteen year-old schoolgirl was attacked whilst on her morning paper round in an underpass below 'Road 50'. The attacker wore a stocking mask and threatened the girl with a Stanley craft knife. He stripped her and committed serious sexual assaults on her, including rape.

Once again, police investigation failed to identify the attacker.

The victims had all given descriptions of their attacker and police knew they were looking for a white man between twenty and thirty years of age. He was between 5' 8" and 6' tall, stocky build and had a 'beer belly'. The attacker had short dark brown hair, a moustache and a small hooped earring. He was softly spoken with a local accent and always casually dressed.

Why the attacks then appear to have stopped is a mystery, although this is not the first time a sex offender had 'retired'. Had he moved away, possibly gone abroad? Or perhaps he had been working on the Laindon development and had been living in 'digs', before returning to his real home. Alternatively, he could have been sent to prison or to a mental institution. Surely people like him don't just stop?

Sometimes they do.

Take the case of The 'Dearne Valley Shoe Rapist', James Lloyd. Between 1983 and 1986, a series of sex attacks occurred on women in South Yorkshire. The attacker sometimes carried stockings and tights with him to use as a mask and to tie up his victims. Late at night he would lay in wait for lone women returning from public houses or clubs, pouncing on them from behind and dragging them into secluded areas to carry out his assaults. Bizarrely, he often took their shoes as trophies and sometimes stole their jewellery. Despite an extensive police investigation, the 'Dearne Valley Shoe Rapist', as he became known, was not identified.

A 'Cold Case' review was later carried out and a full DNA profile of the rapist was developed. Unfortunately, he was not on the National DNA Database (NDNAD). An appeal was made on Crimewatch, but Lloyd was not among the three hundred and fifty names suggested by callers.

But the net finally began to close in on the rapist when investigators decided to use 'Familial DNA Searching', first successfully used during the M3 lorry driver homicide investigation.

A search of the NDNAD produced a list of 43 people who might be related to the rapist. Third on the list was Lloyd's sister who had given a DNA sample following her arrest for a drink-driving offence. In 2006, she was visited by detectives and interviewed about her family; they learnt that she had a brother James and the officers left having obtained his full details.

James Lloyd was then a forty nine year-old married man living in a luxury home near Barnsley, together with his wife and their children. Lloyd was Works Manager at Dearne Valley Printers Ltd., in Wath-on-Dearne, near Rotherham. A long-standing Freemason, he was described as a 'pillar of society'.

Unfortunately, after police had left her, Lloyd's sister contacted her brother and told him that the police would be visiting him in order to request a voluntary DNA sample. Following that telephone call, Lloyd panicked and called his father telling him he had once committed some serious offences. Lloyd asked his father to look after his children as he was going to commit suicide. Fortunately, the suicide attempt was thwarted when one of his children returned home to find his father trying to hang himself.

A DNA sample subsequently obtained from Lloyd linked him to three of the attacks and he was arrested in April 2006. He told the officers, 'I knew that was coming. I was a bastard 20 years ago.'

Enquiries revealed that at the time of the rapes, Lloyd was also working as a part time taxi driver and would often be out late at night. His first marriage had ended in divorce and in 1985 he re-married; and it may be of some significance that the attacks ceased soon after.

When police searched his workplace they found a trap door to which only Lloyd had the key. This led to a hidden compartment in which was found bags containing more than 100 pairs of stiletto shoes, plus new and worn stockings and tights. Police also found a document called 'The Perfect Victim', which described the trussing up and raping of women in the same way that Lloyd had carried out his attacks. However, it was not clear if Lloyd had written this himself.

Lloyd later pleaded guilty to four rapes and two attempted rapes, although police suspected that he may have attacked more women. He was sentenced to life imprisonment. The trial judge said Lloyd would serve a minimum of fourteen and a half years before he could be considered for release. However, the Court of Appeal later reduced the recommended minimum term to seven years and 263 days.

The fact that Lloyd appears to have ceased his attacks after getting married suggests that 'a leopard can change his spots'. Perhaps the 'Laindon Rapist' had also settled down?

During the late 1990's, the DNA profiles of the Laindon Rapist were loaded onto the NDNAD. They would now be routinely checked against any new DNA profiles going onto the database. The hope was that, like Wayne Doherty, the Laindon Rapist will eventually come to police notice in circumstances that would result in his DNA being obtained, profiled, searched and matched to the attacks.

In 2004, the forensic aspects of the Laindon Rapes investigations were reviewed by the 'Cold Case' Team. We recommended that further enquiries were carried out utilising the opportunities presented via 'Familial DNA Searching'. To date these have proved unsuccessful, but will no doubt be tried again in the future.

The attacks have twice been featured on BBC TV's Crimewatch programme, the last time being in 2008. During the twenty four hour period following the broadcast, over two hundred calls were received from around the country. Some came from other rape victims; other callers gave names of possible suspects. All were followed up, but none led to the Laindon Rapist being identified.

In advance of the last television screening, two of the victims spoke about their respective ordeals. The first, attacked in December 1991, said she regularly felt guilt over what had happened to her. She said that if she had hurt him, he may have been caught and this might have prevented his last attack.

The incident, she said, had affected her life. She no longer wears skirts and now 'dresses down' to make herself less attractive to any potential attacker. But she was still willing to give evidence against her attacker to show him that she is not a 'crumbling wreck'. Defiantly, she said, 'He has no control or power over me.'

His final victim told reporters that for a long time after the attack she was frightened of being alone, suffered flashbacks and recurring nightmares. She went on to say that not a day goes by when she does not think about what he did to her; and that she has never achieved closure because he was never caught.

The Senior Investigating Officer, Detective Superintendent John Quinton, spoke of his officers' determination to eventually catch this rapist.

And perhaps one day he will be caught. That way his victims can achieve some peace of mind, albeit they will never forget what happened to them.

It only takes a phone call from someone who has their suspicions about a particular individual and the police can do the rest. The science of DNA has ensured that innocent suspects can be quickly and easily eliminated from this investigation.

CHAPTER 20
CONCLUSIONS

Essex Police has enjoyed some real success as a result of their reviews of previously unsolved major crimes, especially murder and 'Stranger Rape'. Some of the criminals who committed those historic crimes still posed a risk to the public at the time of their arrest; consequently, their subsequent conviction and imprisonment has made Essex a much safer place for all who live and / or work here.

Unfortunately it is not always possible to identify and then to convict all those who committed serious crimes many years ago. However, as we have seen, it is often possible to make real progress with an old investigation, progress that may one day lead to its final resolution. This is particularly so in relation to those suspects whose DNA profiles have now been developed and are currently sitting on the National DNA Database awaiting identification. For those suspects it is not just important that they keep out of trouble, but that their blood relatives (over whose behaviour they probably have little or no control) must also keep out of trouble, lest their DNA profiles one day indirectly lead police to their doorstep.

The day-to-day work on specific cases continues to be carried out behind closed doors and few people will be aware of the progress that is being, or has already been made. However, when I retired in 2014, I began to have some real concern about the future of 'Cold Case' work. I am happy to voice my concerns, but should make it clear that I am not representing the views of police service generally, nor of Essex Police in particular. Neither am I, necessarily, representing the views of ex-colleagues, although I believe some may share my concerns.

The first of my concerns related to the closure of the Forensic Science Service (FSS) in 2012. At that time the FSS was a government-owned company which provided forensic science services to the police forces and government agencies of England and Wales. Their 'customers' also included the Crown Prosecution Service, HM Revenue and Customs, HM Coroners' Service and both the Ministry of Defence and British Transport Police forces.

The FSS had seven main laboratories throughout the country, each one serving one or more local police forces and other agencies. But, in addition, some laboratories also specialised in particular aspects of forensic science, for example, document examination, firearms and explosives, etc.

Over decades, FSS staff acquired considerable knowledge and experience in the particular areas of forensic science in which they worked. They had successfully used this to research and develop further advances in forensic science. For example, the FSS pioneered the use of large scale DNA profiling for forensic identification and crime detection, and set up the world's first national DNA Database which was launched in 1995.

When the government first announced the impending closure of the FSS, they cited as the justification for closure, monthly losses of up to two million pounds. However, in my view, closure was a bad decision as the FSS was an important public service, just as the NHS is; and it deserved a similar level of support and protection. Now, all that really remains of the FSS is the Archive. This is the national collection of old case files and retained casework samples, such as microscope slides, fibre and other potentially important materials. These have been kept to assist the reviews of 'Cold Cases' and the conduct of appeals, etc.

However, any forensic work that now has to be carried out in respect of these (and current investigations) is contracted out to the private sector, or carried out by the police service, etc., 'in-house'.

Senior politicians, scientists and lawyers warned that closing the FSS Archive would cause miscarriages of justice and stop police solving crimes, as police forces now had to create individual storage systems.

Most private sector forensic science laboratories do a good job; and so they should as many former FSS staff are now employed within them. However, like any other private company they are primarily in business to make a profit. Consequently, the amount of money the police can spend on forensic science work is limited as a significant proportion of that expenditure now goes towards the private companies' profits.

Because of the situation they now find themselves in, investigators, whether dealing with a simple car theft or a murder, can no longer commission all the forensic work they once would have requested. And whilst the police service, etc., has acquired some expertise in the examination of certain forensic material 'in house', it is difficult to see how they can ever enjoy the same degree of confidence that the more independent FSS once enjoyed.

I was therefore please to hear, quite recently, that the creation of a new forensic and biometrics service is now being considered by the Home Office. This follows concerns voiced by the National Audit Office who had warned in a report, that standards were slipping. The report came only three years after forensic science work had been transferred from the FSS to private laboratories and in-house police laboratories. The report's authors concluded that forensic science provision was now under threat because police were increasingly relying on unregulated experts to examine samples from suspects and crime scenes.

In its plan, the Home Office acknowledged that forensic science provision had become fragmented. In particular, the digital analysis of computers and smart-phones was being conducted in an 'ad hoc manner' which did not provide value for money. Ministers said they were supporting a police review of whether there should be a 'joint Forensic and Biometric Service' to achieve economies of scale, increased capability and resilience.

Linked to my concerns about the closure of the FSS were my concerns about the possible consequences of the government's Comprehensive Spending Review. During the past few years police budgets, in real terms, have been cut significantly; and more cuts are currently threatened. As most of the police budget is spent on personnel, the only way to achieve significant cuts in spending is to reduce staffing levels. Most senior police officers and politicians know this; but many still try to assure the public that no matter what the cuts, it will still be 'business as usual'. In particular, they say that the 'front line' will not be affected as any such cuts will be made in the 'back office'.

Now I for one, would like to find that 'back office' where dozens of police officers and support staff sit around doing nothing useful all day; but it does not exist! 'Cold Case' Reviewers are examples of 'back office' workers as we do not work on the so called 'front line'. Therefore, if financial cuts lead to further reductions in the numbers of support staff employed, who will now do this and other important work? I am not suggesting that the police service will completely withdraw from 'Cold Case' work, but I anticipate that in the foreseeable future, fewer staff and less finance will be allocated to this important and demanding area of criminal investigation.

Despite my concerns, I still believe that that a few people reading this book will now be dreading the knock on their front door which will come on that day when their own past finally catches up with them. As previously stated, they always have the option of pre-empting that visit by going to the police and facing up to their crimes, some of which were committed many years ago when they were different people, leading totally different lives.

Hopefully, others will read this book and find the courage to share with the police, what they know about a particular unsolved crime. Anything they say will always be in dealt with in confidence and both the police and courts now have tried and tested procedures in place to protect any witnesses who feel they may be at risk if they go to the police. But if an individual really cannot face going to the police, they can pass their information anonymously via Crimestoppers on 0800 555 111.

Crimestoppers is an independent, registered charity that was set up many years ago to receive information about crime and criminals. If the caller wishes to remain anonymous, not even their sex is revealed to the police; and calls to Crimestoppers cannot be traced. Rewards are often given and can be paid out without the caller ever having to reveal their true identity.

The information given to Crimestoppers is then forwarded to the appropriate police force or other agency. Crimestoppers also has a system which invites the caller to re-contact them about their previous call(s), for example, if they wish to give further information or receive an update on the investigation of the information they previously gave.

To those who have important information about serious crimes or criminals I would say that, for the benefit of the society of which you are a part, and for the victims of all such crimes and their families, you must share that information with the police. The next victim of the person you suspect could be you, a member of your family, one of your friends or some other innocent or vulnerable person. And if it is, it will be no good wishing you had acted earlier. You will then have to live with the knowledge that someone else became a victim because of your silence or that you helped someone get away with a murder or rape; or perhaps that you prevented the body of a missing person from being returned to their family and finally laid to rest.

We cannot always prevent individuals from becoming victims. But if they are, we should all do our best to ensure that those responsible are held to account for their crimes and that those left behind are better able to get on with their lives.

The End

About the Author

Ray Newman was born in Walthamstow, London, and educated at the Sidney Chaplin Secondary Modern School. He left school in 1962 at the age of 15 with no qualifications; something he says he very quickly came to regret! Ray went into the 'rag trade' working at a local shirt factory where he remained for nearly ten years. During this time, Ray became a Special Constable at Walthamstow (Metropolitan Police Service) leaving in 1970 when he got married and moved to Essex.

In 1972, Ray joined the then Essex & Southend-on-Sea Joint Constabulary (now Essex Police). He served all around the county in uniform and CID, in all ranks up to and including Temporary Superintendent. During this time Ray also gained a Diploma in Criminology from the University of London and a Bachelor of Arts Degree with the Open University. He is a Member of the Chartered Management Institute.

In 2002, Ray retired as a police officer, but soon rejoined Essex Police as a member of the support staff, initially working as an Assistant Investigating Officer. Then, in 2003, he became a founder member of the newly formed Major Crime Review Team where he remained until his eventual retirement in 2014. During this time he was also an Associate Lecturer in Forensic Science the South East Essex College.

However, unable to completely retire, Ray, together with two associates, set up a Review and Investigations consultancy, BWC Solutions Ltd. (www.bwcsolutions.co.uk) He is also a part-time Associate Mental Health Act Hospital Manager and a volunteer Community First Responder with the East of England Ambulance Service. In his spare time Ray gives talks and lectures on 'Cold Cases' and other police related subjects.

Ray is married with four grown up children, one of whom is an Essex Police dog handler. Two of his other children are teachers and the fourth is in catering. Together with his wife Ann, a retired paediatric nurse, he still lives in Essex.

Contact Ray via rmnbooks@btinternet.com

Printed in Great Britain
by Amazon

63402781R00112